A.S.J. TESSIMOND
COLLECTED POEMS

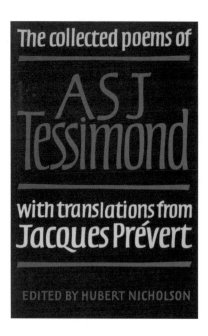

The collected poems of
A S J
Tessimond
with translations from
Jacques Prévert
EDITED BY HUBERT NICHOLSON

This book is a reissue of the original *Collected Poems* of A.S.J. Tessimond, published by the Whiteknights Press at the University of Reading in 1985. This was designed by students in the university's Department of Typography & Graphic Communication, and set in Linotype-Paul Trump Mediæval. The original cover with hand-drawn lettering by Caroline Webb is reproduced above. There was also a special limited edition signed by Hubert Nicholson and bound in calf by George Miller.

ASJ TESSIMOND
COLLECTED POEMS

with translations from **Jacques Prévert**

EDITED BY HUBERT NICHOLSON

BLOODAXE BOOKS
WHITEKNIGHTS PRESS

ISBN: 978 1 85224 857 4

First published 1985 by
Whiteknights Press.

This edition first published 2010 by
Bloodaxe Books Ltd,
Highgreen,
Tarset,
Northumberland NE48 1RP,
in association with
Whiteknights Press,
an imprint of the University of Reading,
Faculty of Arts and Humanities, Whiteknights,
Reading, Berkshire RG6 6AA.

www.bloodaxebooks.com
For further information about Bloodaxe titles
please visit our website or write to
the above address for a catalogue.

Supported by
ARTS COUNCIL
ENGLAND

Typesetting: Whiteknights Press (see previous page).

Cover design: Neil Astley & Pamela Robertson-Pearce.

Printed in Great Britain by
Bell & Bain Limited, Glasgow, Scotland.

CONTENTS

CONTENTS

CONTENTS

Poems first collected in *Selection* (1947–57)

CONTENTS

Poems first collected in *Not love perhaps ...*

Poems first collected in *Morning meeting*

Poems hitherto uncollected

Translations from the French of Jacques Prévert

CONTENTS

NOTE ON SOURCES

This volume brings together all A. S. J. Tessimond's work that has appeared in book form[1] and some twenty-seven original poems and twenty-five translations hitherto unpublished or uncollected.

Three volumes were published during the poet's lifetime: *The walls of glass* (Methuen, 1934), *Voices in a giant city* (Heinemann, 1947), and *Selection* (Putnam, 1958). There have been two posthumous selections, both edited by Hubert Nicholson: *Not love perhaps ...* (Autolycus Publications, 1978) and *Morning meeting* (Autolycus Publications, 1980).

Of the previously uncollected material in the present volume, four of the translations from the French of Jacques Prévert and some seventeen of his own poems were first published in periodicals during the poet's lifetime, the earliest when he was twenty-four. Details are as follows:

The New Age: The pathetic fallacy (27 May, 1926); Symphony in red (25 November, 1926); Charleston (7 April, 1927); Soliloquy of the artists (22 March, 1928).

The New Coterie: The conductor (Summer-Autumn, 1927).

Poetry: Lines (vol. 32, no. 1, April 1928); Portrait (vol. 47, no. 4, January 1936).

This Quarter: Authorship; Man; A painting by Seurat (vol. 1, no. 3, 1928); Sleep; The train (vol. 1, no. 4, 1929).

The Fortnightly Review: Dancing (July, 1935).

Life and Letters: Latter-day oracles: Noise (vol. 14, no. 3, Spring 1936).

Twentieth Century Verse: In that cold land; To a lover of living (no. 1, January 1937).

Delta: Conversation with a disembodied spirit (no. 18, Summer 1959).

The London Magazine: Three Prévert translations: Quicksands; When children are in love; Song of the gaoler (September 1956).

Encounter: Prévert translation: Paris by night (June 1958).

Of the poems printed in the earlier collections, many appeared

---

1 Except for some quatrains for children accompanying the illustrations in an edition of *Bewick's birds* (Hutchinson, 1952).

first in the pages of some of the **above** or in the following publications: *Adelphi*; *Du* (Zurich); *European Caravan*; *Horizon*; *Listener*; *London Mercury*; *Modern Writing*; *New English Weekly*; *New Statesman*; *New Yorker*; *Orion*; *Penguin New Writing*; *Programme* (Oxford); *Seed*; *Spectator*; *Sunday Times*; *Tambour* (Paris); *Time and Tide*; *The Times*; *Times Literary Supplement*; *transition* (Paris); *Truth*; *Weekend Review*.

Tessimond's poems have been broadcast in England, Ireland, Australia, Canada and South Africa, as well as by BBC External Services. Some have been used as test-pieces at various festivals and contests, have appeared in numerous school textbooks, and are to be found in many well-known anthologies, including *New signatures* (Hogarth, 1932); *New country* (Hogarth, 1933); *Poems of our time, 1900–42* (Everyman); *Poems of the war years* (Macmillan); *The terrible rain* (Methuen, 1966); *The centuries' poetry, 5* (Penguin, 1938); *Poetry 1934–50* (Longmans Green, for the British Council); *The Guinness book of poetry* (1959–60, Putnam); the P.E.N. *New poems, 1952* (Michael Joseph); and *The Oxford book of twentieth-century English verse* (1973).

The British Council tape-recorded Tessimond reading seventeen of his poems, and his work is still constantly broadcast and anthologised in Britain and abroad.

Grateful acknowledgement is tendered to all the above-named publishers and publications. The present editor also feels the warmest gratitude to Mr Jonathan Barker, Arts Council librarian, and Mr Geoffrey Soar, of the library of University College, London, for their invaluable help in tracing Tessimond poems in the 'little magazines' of half a century ago, and to a pioneer in that hunt, Mrs Jean Cooper.

INTRODUCTION

In the two decades since the death of A. S. J. Tessimond, the conviction
has grown stronger that his was not only a rich individual talent but
one of the authentic and significant voices of his time. This opinion
is not founded on the mere fact that a handful of his poems continue
to be anthologised and broadcast, here and abroad, nor is it the
partiality of one who enjoyed the poet's personal friendship for the
last twenty years of his life. Others besides myself, men and women
of literary judgment, and many a common reader would concur.

His hallmark, his unique contribution to the body-poetic, is to be
found in those poems encapsulating urban types – the man in the
bowler hat, the man in the saloon bar or the dance hall, the
psychiatrist, the ad-man, the prostitute, the 'man of culture', the
neurotic, the lesser artist, the girl who wants to be a cynic, the
romantic, the hypochondriac – and the institutions that shape and
demarcate their lives, the popular press and radio, films, money,
advertising, machines, houses, tube stations, the implacable streets.
Who else of this era has so acutely observed these phenomena, or
made such thoughtful, witty, lucid poetry out of them, has listened
with so sensitive an ear to the 'voices in a giant city'? Who has so
penetrated the heart of London, 'city of two divided cities', whose
'tears fall inward', or indeed that of England (1938), 'the snail that's
shod with lightning ... Shall we laugh or shall we weep?' But this
historical or documentary value would be nothing were not the poems
themselves beautiful, shapely, well wrought and elegant, whether in
public or private mode.

And as will be seen, in the two hundred or so poems here brought
together, such were by no means his only themes. He wrote a good
deal about love, its hopes and ecstasies and its frustrations and sadness.
As a man, he was forever falling in love afresh: a long succession of
never wholly consummated passions, the last psychological barrier
never passed. He died a bachelor, without offspring, but he wrote
touchingly and not always blindly about the girls he adored.

He has a number of poems beginning 'I am', but they are not in
the least egotistical. They are imaginative projections of himself into
types, places, generalised Man, even God or Fate.

Tessimond was entirely a man of the city. His 'landscape' pieces depict Hyde Park Corner, Chelsea Embankment, a Paris café. Even from Jamaica he brought back only the interior landscape of an overcrowded bus. Birds, beasts and flowers were in general beyond his poetic ken, even though his possibly best-known poem is about cats. He certainly had some fellow-feeling for cats, which 'no less liquid than their shadows / Offer no angles to the wind' and cannot be truly possessed. But he never kept a cat, or any other pet. He was no animal-lover; and as for children, they rather frightened him. But he loved the life around him and was a meditative as well as an observant man. He reflected, and reflected on, the passing show, kindly, honestly, and with wit and wisdom.

The word 'conversation' occurs in the titles of several poems – 'Middle-aged conversation', 'Conversation for three', 'Conversation with a disembodied spririt', 'Conversation with myself' – and it is a pointer to his character, for good talk was one of his delights.

Arthur Seymour John Tessimond – Jack to his family and youthful companions, John in adult life – was born in Birkenhead on July 19, 1902, only child of a bank inspector. His mother's maiden name was Evans, so there may have been a Welsh strain. He felt misunderstood and unloved by his parents, and relied for human warmth on a kindly old aunt. (She lived to ninety, and left him some money.) It was to his feeling of being starved of maternal affection that psychiatrists later attributed his sexual difficulties, a diagnosis that did nothing to effect a cure.

In appearance he was tall, slim, fair, well mannered and precise of speech, handsome in youth, haggard in later years. He was a more sociable man than he chose to think himself. He loved dancing and night life, went to many parties, read his verse often to the Epsom Poetry Circle, even took part in amateur theatricals (impersonating Coleridge in Peacock's 'Nightmare Abbey').

At the age of fourteen, Tessimond went to Charterhouse. At sixteen, according to his own account, he refused to go back to school[1] and ran away to London with the idea of earning his living as a free-lance journalist, with, of course, no experience, no worldly knowledge, no qualification and no flair for journalism. It was a boyish dream. As he said in a letter to me years later, he found he 'hadn't the guts to try for more than a fortnight, after which time I let myself be trotted back to Birkenhead.' After a year of doing 'nothing in particular', he went to Liverpool University, where he studied for four years, during which time he became engaged to be married.

1 Frances Richards, in her pamphlet 'A friendship with John Tessimond', says he was expelled, 'for something someone else had done.'

Not a particularly early developer, he was in his twenties when he
began to get his poems into print. At some point he wrote to Ezra
Pound, evidently enclosing some of his poems and a critical article
he had written (now lost) about G.B.S., and asking advice on markets
for his work. He received a characteristically scabrous reply, typed
with a very faint ribbon, uncorrected, and without sender's address
or date. This was evidently before 1928, for in that year the Seurat
poem mentioned appeared in *This Quarter*.

Helpful, though in a grudging fashion, Pound being Pound –
Tessimond spoke of it rather ruefully – it runs as follows:

> Dear Sir:
> If you were in the least familiar with my work you wd.
> know what I think of criticism in general & not try to arouse
> my interest with a perfectly innocuous specimen of same.
> Also you wd. know that I think Shaw simple shit, with no
> base, and not pick that particular bit of revery. Of course I
> think all England chiefly shit, and none of Shaw's generation
> capable of serious thought, or even mental honesty.
> Thank gawd I am out of the world of letters, editorial
> functions. etc.
> Painting by Seurat, might get into 'Poetry', 232 East
> Erie St, Chicago.
> Double Dealer, 204 Baronne St. New Orleans.
> To want to appear in Dial is ambition à rebours.
> The Criterion belongs to an epoch I dimly remember.
> I believe Mr Walsh is bringing out a Quarterly in Paris
> (I haven't yet seen a copy),[1] with active intentions; also
> Mr Edwin Seaver, Woodstock, Ulster Co., N.Y.
> Also the 'Guardian' Phila.
> Cant see that yr. work has any marked individuality, or as
> yet any character to distinguish it from anyone elses. England
> has gone to hell, and if you are determined to write you had
> better go somewhere else, as you will get nothing but carion
> [sic] and pus from your surroundings, weekly prints etc.
> It is rubbish to say you have to know an editor personally
> (it is true of Bloomsbury and a few pustular cliques), many
> editors perfer [sic] not to know their contributors. The
> Munro-e-s Arold and Arriet are perfectly open minded towards
> strangers, i,e, with what minds they've got.
> As you dont inclose autobiography, I cant tell yr. age, etc.
> I can not overemphasize the degree to which I think England
> (so called lit. and intellect. life) gone to hell, pustulent, etc.

1 *This Quarter* (October 1925 – June 1932), the third issue. The first issue had been
dedicated to Ezra Pound, but in the third issue, after Ernest Walsh's death, his successor
as editor, Ethel Moorhead, retracted the dedication. This yields a probable date of
1925 for Pound's letter.
'A painting by Seurat', the poem Pound refers to earlier in the letter, appeared in
This Quarter in that same third issue, so his advice may have been heeded, perhaps.

INTRODUCTION

> If you want to write (etc) Aldington is honest, and Wyndham
> Lewis (not the punk writing in the D.M.) is a man of genius.
> Monro is also honest. You must be very much out of the
> world to have invoked me ... from oltre tomba ...
>   impression of yr. work neutral. If you can write a whole
> book ... you can possibly get some attention ... 'Poetry' the
> magazine is as good a pepiniere[1] as you need for stray verse.
> Dont come back to me until you have gone at least far enough
> in your study of literary values to be cured of talking about
> Shaw in what I presume you mean for a serious article.
>
>   E.P.

Scrawled on the back of this letter in pencil, in Pound's large
handwriting, are the words: 'Not hopeless if you are less than 21.'
Tessimond was then 23.

A study of the 'little magazines' of the late 1920s and early 1930s
shows Tessimond to have been assiduous in marketing his poems in
London, Paris, Monte Carlo, Chicago, New York. (Not, however, in
the *Dial*!) He had no agent.

Later on, he was rather severe in discarding early poems, as 'infantile
cluckings and bubblings.' But he sustained a quiet confidence in
himself as literary artist, diligently working over and above all
clarifying his verses – he abhorred obscurity. Perhaps he should have
been born French, being a natural boulevardier, a true Francophil,
and a poetic craftsman of Gallic precision and irony. He felt a strong
affinity with Jacques Prévert, of whose work he made the twenty-five
translations printed, mostly for the first time, in this volume.
Tessimond was no Baudelaire, but he conformed to some degree to
that poet's celebrated vision of creative dandyism, which 'borders
upon the spiritual and stoical', with 'latent fires which could not
choose but to burst into flame'. He had a touch of the *flâneur*, and
knew, like the French poets, the fascinations of the wicked city. But
of course he was no elegant idler plucking *fleurs du mal*: he had his
living to earn.

To revert to his career: his first job on leaving university was as
a teacher, but two terms sufficed to convince him that was not his
métier. He wrote around vainly for other jobs he saw advertised:
cinema manager, information officer, bank clerk, and even reader to
a blind old man. He had poems published in the *Listener* and John
Middleton Murry's magazine, the *Adelphi*. His talent attracted local
attention, and in 1927, when he was twenty-five, he was awarded
the Felicia Hemans Prize for Poetry. (Mrs Hemans, author of

1 Pépinière: *nursery-garden.*

[xvi]

Casabianca, 'The boy stood on the burning deck', had been a Liverpool woman.)

His engagement at an end, he finally made the break from his home and went to live in London, where his new love worked. The novelist Olaf Stapledon had given him some literary introductions there, but nothing came of them.

For two years he worked in London bookshops, and then became an advertising copywriter. His opinions of that trade can be seen in his posthumously published poem 'The ad-man' and the rather backhanded 'Defence of the ad-man' here printed for the first time. He nevertheless practised it quite successfully for the rest of his life, apart from the comically-disastrous wartime interlude. When war came he decided he would be not only 'intensely miserable' as a soldier but 'useless and even dangerous to others'. So he gave up his job and his flat, and tried to live under cover, with the aid of friends, avoiding the call-up. When finally he submitted to his medical, he was rejected as unfit!

Advertising brought him some interesting and congenial colleagues, among them the Welsh painter Ceri Richards. Together they composed in 1930 though never published an illustrated alphabet of advertising, of which a sample may suffice:

> K for kaleidoscope – the many-coloured criss-cross of the
> world shaken this morning by the hand of today: in which
> advertising picks out the pattern that is fashion; deciphering
> it and using it subtly for the seller's advantage.

Ceri and his artist-wife Frances affectionately befriended Tessimond from 1928 to the end of his life, and she has written how three days before his death she took food and money to his Chelsea flat, he having given everything away to his latest girl-friend. Frances Richards was Tessimond's favourite artist, along with Modigliani, with whom she perhaps has something in common, in her manner of formalising human and natural appearances.

Tessimond's poetic beginnings were strongly influenced by Imagism, which may be one of the reasons why he wrote to Pound, the father-figure of that short-lived movement. 'Cats' is self-evidently an Imagist poem. But he was quickly his own man, and quite unlike any other (*pace* Pound). He had an obvious joy in versification. As well as free verse, he used skilfully a great variety of stanza-form, metre, length of line and rhyme-scheme. You may find a rhymed twelve-line poem using only two rhymes throughout ('Conversation with myself') or lines of eight stresses and up to twenty-three syllables ('After attempted escape from love'). Someone has affirmed that 'Black

Monday lovesong' is the first poem since 'Hiawatha' to put its dancing rhythm of trochaic dimeters to serious use. Tessimond also liked patterns on the page, anticipating more recent fashions. Thus 'Sleep (II)' is a literal illustration of the metaphor 'falling asleep'.

Tessimond's father left him about four thousand pounds, a sum not to be sneezed at in 1945. He spent half of it on his nightclub hostesses, striptease girls and models, and the other half on 'four or five successive psycho-analysts', for by the onset of middle age he had become gravely manic-depressive. In the depth of his depressions he often contemplated and talked of suicide, but never actually attempted it.

In the final phase of his life he underwent electric shock therapy at ever-shortening intervals. This had a deleterious effect on his memory, though not on his intellect. It temporarily raised his spirits to a rather hectic pitch, and may or may not have staved off self-destruction. Perhaps it may also have shortened his life.

On May 15, 1962, he was found dead in his flat in Chelsea, from natural causes, a brain haemorrhage, some two months before his sixtieth birthday. He had apparently been dead for two days before his body was discovered. Old age, which he had always feared, was never to be his.

Here, except for some chaff and juvenilia, is all his poetry.

Hubert Nicholson

The walls of glass

Any man speaks

I, after difficult entry through my mother's blood
And stumbling childhood (hitting my head against the world);
I, intricate, easily unshipped, untracked, unaligned;
Cut off in my communications; stammering; speaking
A dialect shared by you, but not you and you;
I, strangely undeft, bereft; I searching always
For my lost rib (clothed in laughter yet understanding)
To come round the corner of Wardour Street into the Square
Or to signal across the Park and share my bed;
I, focus in night for star-sent beams of light,
I, fulcrum of levers whose ends I cannot see ...
Have this one deftness – that I admit undeftness:
Know that the stars are far, the levers long:
Can understand my unstrength.

Nursery-rhyme for a twenty-first birthday

You cannot see the walls that divide your hand
From his or hers or mine when you think you touch it.

You cannot see the walls because they are glass,
And glass is nothing until you try to pass it.

Beat on it if you like, but not too hard,
For glass will break you even while you break it.

Shout, and the sound will be broken and driven backwards,
For glass, though clear as water, is deaf as granite.

This fraudulent inhibition is cunning: wise men
Content themselves with breathing patterns on it.

Never

Suddenly, desperately
I thought, 'No, never
In millions of minutes
Can I for one second
Calm-leaving my own self
Like clothes on a chair-back
And quietly opening
The door of one house
(No, not one of all millions)
Of blood, flesh and brain,
Climb the nerve-stair and look
From the tower, from the windows
Of eyes not my own: ...
No, never, no, never!'

Houses

People who are afraid of themselves
Multiply themselves into families
And so divide themselves
And so become less afraid.

People who might have to go out
Into clanging strangers' laughter,
Crowd under roofs, make compacts
To no more than smile at each other.

People who might meet their own faces
Or surprise their own voices in doorways
Build themselves rooms without mirrors
And live between walls without echoes.

People who might meet other faces
And unknown voices round corners
Build themselves rooms all mirrors
And live between walls all echoes.

People who are afraid to go naked
Clothe themselves in families, houses,
But are still afraid of death
Because death one day will undress them.

The children look at the parents

We being so hidden from those who
Have quietly borne and fed us,
How can we answer civilly
Their innocent invitations?

How can we say, 'we see you
As but-for-God's-grace-ourselves, as
Our caricatures (we yours), with
Time's telescope between us'?

How can we say 'you presumed on
The accident of kinship,
Assumed our friendship coatlike,
Not as a badge one fights for'?

How say 'and you remembered
The sins of our outlived selves and
Your own forgiveness, buried
The hatchet to slow music;

Shared money but not your secrets;
Will leave as your final legacy
A box double-locked by the spider
Packed with your unsolved problems'?

How say all this without capitals,
Italics, anger or pathos,
To those who have seen from the womb come
Enemies? How not say it?

Meeting

Dogs take new friends abruptly and by smell.
Cats' meetings are neat, tactual, caressive.
Monkeys exchange their fleas before they speak.
Snakes, no doubt, coil by coil reach mutual knowledge.

We then, at first encounter, should be silent;
Not court the cortex but the epidermis;
Not work from inside out but outside in;
Discover each other's flesh, its scent and texture;
Familiarize the sinews and the nerve-ends,
The hands, the hair – before the inept lips open.

Instead of which we are resonant, explicit.
Our words like windows intercept our meaning.
Our four eyes fence and flinch and awkwardly
Wince into shadow, slide oblique to ambush.
Hands stir, retract. The pulse is insulated.
Blood is turned inwards, lonely; skin unhappy ...
While always under all, but interrupted,
Antennæ stretch ... waver ... and almost ... touch.

Chaplin

The sun, a heavy spider, spins in the thirsty sky.
The wind hides under cactus leaves, in doorway corners. Only the wry

Small shadow accompanies Hamlet-Petrouchka's march – the slight
Wry sniggering shadow in front in the morning,
    turning at noon, behind towards night.

The plumed cavalcade has passed to to-morrow, is lost again;
But the wisecrack-mask, the quick-flick-fanfare of the cane remain.

Diminuendo of footsteps even is done:
Only remain, Don Quixote, hat, cane, smile and sun.

Goliaths fall to our sling, but craftier fates than these
Lie ambushed – malice of open manholes, strings in the dark and
    falling trees.

God kicks our backsides, scatters peel on the smoothest stair;
And towering centaurs steal the tulip lips, the aureoled hair,

While we, craned from the gallery, throw our cardboard flowers
And our feet jerk to tunes not played for ours.

Don Juan

Under the lips and limbs, the embraces, faces,
Under the sharp circumference, the brightness,
Under the fence of shadows,
Is something I am seeking;
Under the faces a face,
Under the new an old or a not-yet-come-to;
Under the voices a peace.

Am I a darkness all your flames must light?
A mirror all your eyes must look into –
That dares not yet reflect the neutral sky,
The empty eye of the sky?

One almost might

Wouldn't you say,
Wouldn't you say: one day,
With a little more time or a little more patience, one might
Disentangle for separate, deliberate, slow delight
One of the moment's hundred strands, unfray
Beginnings from endings, this from that, survey
Say a square inch of the ground one stands on, touch
Part of oneself or a leaf or a sound (not clutch
Or cuff or bruise but touch with finger-tip, ear-
Tip, eyetip, creeping near yet not too near);
Might take up life and lay it on one's palm
And, encircling it in closeness, warmth and calm,
Let it lie still, then stir smooth-softly, and
Tendril by tendril unfold, there on one's hand ...

One might examine eternity's cross-section
For a second, with slightly more patience, more time for reflection?

Last word to childhood

Ice-cold fear has slowly decreased
As my bones have grown, my height increased.
Though I shiver in snow of dreams, I shall never
Freeze again in a noonday terror.

I shall never break, my sinews crumble
As God-the-headmaster's fingers fumble
At the other side of unopening doors
Which I watch for a hundred thousand years.

I shall never feel my thin blood leak
While darkness stretches a paw to strike
Or Nothing beats an approaching drum
Behind my back in a silent room.

I shall never, alone, meet the end of my world
At the bend of a path, the turn of a wall:
Never, or once more only, and
That will be once and an end of end.

Epitaph for our children

Blame us for these who were cradled and rocked in our chaos;
    Watching our sidelong watching, fearing our fear;
Playing their blind-man's-buff in our gutted mansions,
    Their follow-my-leader on a stair that ended in air.

Unlyric love song

It is time to give that-of-myself which I could not at first:
To offer you now at last my least and my worst:
Minor, absurd preserves,
The shell's end-curves,
A document kept at the back of a drawer,
A tin hidden under the floor,
Recalcitrant prides and hesitations:
To pile them carefully in a desperate oblation
And say to you 'quickly! turn them
Once over and burn them'.

Now I (no communist, heaven knows!
Who have kept as my dearest right to close
My tenth door after I've opened nine to the world,
To unfold nine sepals holding one hard-furled)
Shall – or shall try to – offer to you
A communism of two ...

See, entry's yours;
Here, the last door!

Empty room

The clock disserts on punctuation, syntax.
The clock's voice, thin and dry, asserts, repeats.
The clock insists: a lecturer demonstrating,
Loudly, with finger raised, when the class has gone.

But time flows through the room, light flows through the room
Like someone picking flowers, like someone whistling
Without a tune, like talk in front of a fire,
Like a woman knitting or a child snipping at paper.

Cocoon for a skeleton

Clothes: to compose
The furtive, lone
Pillar of bone
To some repose.

To let hands shirk
Utterance behind
A pocket's blind
Deceptive smirk.

To mask, belie
The undue haste
Of breast for breast
Or thigh for thigh.

To screen, conserve
The pose, when death
Half strips the sheath
And leaves the nerve.

To edit, glose
Lyric desire
And slake its fire
In polished prose.

Betrayal

If a man says half himself in the light, adroit
Way a tune shakes into equilibrium,
Or approximates to a note that never comes:

Says half himself in the way two pencil-lines
Flow to each other and softly separate,
In the resolute way plane lifts and leaps from plane:

Who knows what intimacies our eyes may shout,
What evident secrets daily foreheads flaunt,
What panes of glass conceal our beating hearts?

Or not perhaps mistaken

One could so easily mistake for love
Oneself in a coloured glass
(So, seeming new);
Or exploration
Of a room
(Delight exhausted when the last drawer's opened),
Of a town
(Adventure ended with the last shop-window);
Or one's heart expanding in sunlight and someone
     happening to be near.

Epitaph on a disturber of his times

We expected the violin's finger on the upturned nerve;
   Its importunate cry, too laxly curved:
And you drew us an oboe-outline, clean and acute;
   Unadorned statement, accurately carved.

We expected the screen, the background for reverie
   Which cloudforms usefully weave:
And you built the immaculate, adamant, blue-green steel
   Arch of a balanced wave.

We expected a pool with flowers to diffuse and break
   The child-round face of the mirrored moon:
And you blazed a rock-path, begun near the sun, to be finished
   By the trained and intrepid feet of men.

Earthfast

Architects plant their imagination, weld their poems on rock,
Clamp them to the skidding rim of the world and anchor them down
     to its core;
Leave more than the painter's or poet's snail-bright trail on a friable leaf;
Can build their chrysalis round them – stand in their sculpture's belly.

They see through stone, they cage and partition air, they cross-rig space
With footholds, planks for a dance; yet their maze, their flying trapeze
Is pinned to the centre. They write their euclidean music standing
With a hand on a cornice of cloud, themselves set fast, earth-square.

Cats

I

To walk as you walk, green eye, smiler, not
Even ostentatiously alone but simply
Alone ... arching the back in courteous discourtesy,
Gathering the body as a dancer before an unworthy
Audience, treading earth scantly – a task to be done
And done with, girt (curt introvert) for private
Precise avoidance of the undesired,
Pride-attired, generalissimo
Knife-eyed, bisector of moonshine with indigo
Shadow, scorner of earth-floor, flaunter of
Steel-hard sickle curve against the sky ... !

II

Cats, no less liquid than their shadows,
   Offer no angles to the wind.
They slip, diminished, neat, through loopholes
   Less than themselves; will not be pinned

To rules or routes for journeys; counter
   Attack with non-resistance; twist
Enticing through the curving fingers
   And leave an angered, empty fist.

They wait, obsequious as darkness –
   Quick to retire, quick to return;
Admit no aim or ethics; flatter
   With reservations; will not learn

To answer to their names; are seldom
   Truly owned till shot and skinned.
Cats, no less liquid than their shadows,
   Offer no angles to the wind.

Cinema screen

Light's patterns freeze:
Frost on our faces.
Light's pollen sifts
Through the lids of our eyes ...

Light sinks and rusts
In water; is broken
By glass ... rests
On deserted dust.

Light lies like torn
Paper in corners:
A rock-pool's pledge
Of the sea's return.

Light, wrenched at the edges
By wind, looks down
At itself in wrinkled
Mirrors from bridges.

Light thinly unweaves
Itself through darkness
Like foam's unknotting
Strings in waves ...

Now light is again
Accumulated
Swords against us ...
Now it is gone.

Bells, pool and sleep

Bells overbrim with sound
And spread from cupolas
Out through the shaking air
Endless unbreaking circles
Cool and clear as water.

A stone dropped in the water
Opens the lips of the pool
And starts the unovertaking
Rings, till the pool is full
Of waves as the air of bells.

The deep-sea bell of sleep
Under the pool of the mind
Flowers in concentric circles
Of annihilation till
Both sight and sound die out,
Both pool and bells are quelled.

Polyphony in a cathedral

Music curls
In the stone shells
Of the arches, and rings
Their stone bells.

Music lips
Each cold groove
Of parabolas' laced
Warp and woof,
And lingers round nodes
Of the ribbed roof.

Chords open
Their flowers among
The stone flowers; blossom;
Stalkless hang.

Music

This shape without space,
This pattern without stuff,
This stream without dimension
Surrounds us, flows through us,
But leaves no mark.

This message without meaning,
These tears without eyes,
This laughter without lips
Speaks to us but does not
Disclose its clue.

These waves without sea
Surge over us, smooth us.
These hands without fingers
Close-hold us, caress us.
These wings without birds
Strong-lift us, would carry us
If only the one thread broke.

O

Old women look intently at Nothing when the
    doctor announces a cancer, dark fruit, under
    the shrunk left breast.

Girls' hands hold Nothing when the train sucks their
    men from the platform and scoops them down
    the slipway of rail.

Nothing beats in deafened ears on the empty and
    godless altars of mountain tops.

Nothing is the final strength of the strong: the last
    poison on the crumpling lips of the weak.

To be blind

Is it sounds
              converging,
Sounds
       nearing,
Infringement,
                  impingement,
Impact,
        contact
With surfaces of the sounds
Or surfaces without the sounds:
Diagrams,
          skeletal,
                    strange?

Is it winds
            curling round invisible corners?
Polyphony of perfumes?
Antennae discovering an axis,
                    erecting the architecture of a world?

Is it
      orchestration of the finger-tips,
                              graph of a fugue:
Scaffold for colours:
                colour itself being
                            god?

Discovery

When you are slightly drunk
Things are so close, so friendly.
The road asks to be walked upon,
The road rewards you for walking
With firm upward contact answering your downward contact
Like the pressure of a hand in yours.
You think – this studious balancing
Of right leg while left leg advances, of left while right,
How splendid
Like somebody-or-other-on-a-peak-in-Darien!
How cleverly that seat shapes the body of the girl who sits there.
How well, how skilfully that man there walks towards you,
Arms hanging, swinging, waiting.
You move the muscles of your cheeks,
How cunningly a smile responds.
And now you are actually speaking
Round sounding words
Magnificent
As that lady's hat!

Quickstep

Acknowledge the drum's whisper.
Yield to its velvet
Nudge. Cut a slow air-
Curve. Then dip (hip to hip):
Sway, swing, pedantically
Poise. Now recover,
Converting the coda
To prelude of sway-swing-
Recover.
   Acknowledge
The drum-crack's alacrity –
Acrid exactitude –
Catch it, then slacken,
Then catch at as cat catches
Rat. Trace your graph:
Loop, ellipse. Skirt an air-wall
To bend it and break it –
Thus – so –
As the drum speaks!

June sick room

The birds' shrill fluting
Beats on the pink blind,
Pierces the pink blind
At whose edge fumble the sun's
Fingers till one obtrudes
And stirs the thick motes.
The room is a close box of pink warmth.
The minutes click.
A man picks across the street
With a metal-pointed stick.
Three clocks drop each twelve pennies
On the drum of noon.
The birds end.
A child's cry pricks the hush.
The wind plucks at a leaf.
The birds rebegin.

Seaport

Green sea-tarnished copper
And sea-tarnished gold
Of cupolas.

Sea-runnelled streets
Channelled by salt air
That wears the white stone.

The sunlight-filled cistern
Of a dry-dock. Square shadows.
Sun-slatted smoke above meticulous stooping of cranes.

Water pressed up by ships' prows
Going, coming.

City dust turned
Back by the sea-wind's
Wall.

Tube station

The tube lift mounts,
                    sap in a stem,
And blossoms its load,
                    a black, untidy rose.

The fountain of the escalator
                    curls at the crest,
                                        breaks and scatters
A winnow of men,
                    a sickle of dark spray.

Wet city night

Light drunkenly reels into shadow;
Blurs, slurs uneasily;
Slides off the eyeballs:
The segments shatter.

Tree-branches cut arc-light in ragged
Fluttering wet strips.
The cup of the sky-sign is filled too full;
It slushes wine over.

The street-lamps dance a tarantella
And zigzag down the street:
They lift and fly away
In a wind of lights.

Black on black

Serrations of chimneys
Stone-black perforate
Velvet-black dark.
A tree coils in core of darkness.
My swinging
Hands
Incise the night.
A man slips into a doorway,
Black hole in blackness, and drowns there.
A second man passing traces
The diagram of his steps
On invisible pavement. Rain
Draws black parallel threads
Through the hollow of air.

Flight of stairs

Stairs fly as straight as hawks;
Or else in spirals, curve out of curve, pausing
At a ledge to poise their wings before relaunching.
Stairs sway at the height of their flight
Like a melody in Tristan;
Or swoop to the ground with glad spread of their feathers
Before they close them.

They curiously investigate
The shells of buildings,
A hollow core,
Shell in a shell.

Useless to produce their path to infinity
Or turn it to a moral symbol,
For their flight is ambiguous, upwards or downwards as you please;
Their fountain is frozen,
Their concertina is silent.

Music-hall juggler

My hands have power beyond my hands.
My finger-tips extend, and where they end
You cannot see, only the golden stream
They lace, unfold and hold at bay
Until they shift the invisible axle, sway the hollow cone
Of gold, the tent they make against your eyes.
Rise, fountain, rise
But do not break
Until they wake – the eyes –
From cold surprise!

Birch tree

The birch tree in winter
Leaning over the secret pool
Is Narcissus in love
With the slight white branches,
The slim trunk,
In the dark glass;
But,
Spring coming on,
Is afraid,
And scarfs the white limbs
In green.

Sea

I
(Windless Summer)

Between the glass panes of the sea are pressed
Patterns of fronds, and the bronze tracks of fishes.

II
(Winter)

Foam-ropes lasso the seal-black shiny rocks,
Noosing, slipping and noosing again for ever.

III
(Windy Summer)

Over-sea going, under returning, meet
And make a wheel, a shell, to hold the sun.

Night piece

Climb, claim your shelf-room, far
Packed from inquisitive moon
And cold contagious stars.

Lean out, but look no longer,
No further, than to stir
Night with extended finger.

Now fill the box with light,
Flood full the shining block,
Masonry against night.

Let window, curtain, blind
Soft-sieve and sift and shred
The impertinence of sound.

Now draw the silence up,
A blanket round your ears;
Lay darkness close and sure,
Inverted cup to cup
On your acquiescent eyes:
Dismissing body's last outposted spies.

Epilogue

Why can't you say what you mean straight out in prose?
Well, say it yourself: then say 'It's that, but more,
Or less perhaps, or not that way, or not
That after all.' The meaning of a song
Might be an undernote; this tree might mean
That leaf as much as trunk, branch, other leaves.
And does one know till one begins? And let's
Look over hedges far as eyesight lets us,
Since road's not, surely, road, but road and hedge
And feet and sky and smell of hawthorn, horse-dung.

There is another version of this poem under the title 'Preface to a book of verse'. In the alternative version, first printed in *Morning meeting*, p. 14, the lineation is different and the poem ends with these additional lines:

... all this.
        Say what I mean?
                        When, where,
    which I?

Voices in a giant city

The man in the bowler hat

I am the unnoticed, the unnoticeable man:
The man who sat on your right in the morning train:
The man you looked through like a windowpane:
The man who was the colour of the carriage, the colour
    of the mounting
Morning pipe smoke.

I am the man too busy with a living to live,
Too hurried and worried to see and smell and touch:
The man who is patient too long and obeys too much
And wishes too softly and seldom.

I am the man they call the nation's backbone,
Who am boneless – playable catgut, pliable clay:
The Man they label Little lest one day
I dare to grow.

I am the rails on which the moment passes,
The megaphone for many words and voices:
I am graph, diagram,
Composite face.

I am the led, the easily-fed,
The tool, the not-quite-fool,
The would-be-safe-and-sound,
The uncomplaining bound,
The dust fine-ground,
Stone-for-a-statue waveworn pebble-round.

Song in a saloon bar

We are here for fear we think of
  Things that we would rather not;
We are here lest we remember –
  But we have forgotten what;

Here we need not judge, decipher,
  Justify or understand,
And we fathom nothing deeper
  Than the half-pint in our hand;

Here we turn from shadows' questions –
  Who we have been, will be, are –
To the comfortable voices
  Telling stories in the bar;

Here we turn from ghosts and, turning,
  Turn the amber, honey-bright,
Frosted-gold or copper-tawny
  Glassful in the smoky light;

Somewhere yesterday-tomorrow's
  Closing like two closing claws,
But, in here, each mild-and-bitter
  Makes the cunning clock-hands pause;

Let us cluster and stand closer
  Lest we've room to turn and run;
Time for one more round, old man, for ...
  Time for, time for ... one, for one ...

We are here for fear we think of
  Things that we would rather not;
We are here lest we remember –
  But we have forgotten what.

London

I am the city of two divided cities
Where the eyes of rich and poor collide and wonder;
Where the beggar's voice is low and unexpectant,
And in clubs the feet of the servants are soft on the carpet
And the world's wind scarcely stirs the leaves of *The Times*.

I am the reticent, the private city,
The city of lovers hiding wrapped in shadows,
The city of people sitting and talking quietly
Beyond shut doors and walls as thick as a century,
People who laugh too little and too loudly,
Whose tears fall inward, flowing back to the heart.

I am the city whose fog will fall like a finger gently
Erasing the anger of angles, the strident indecorous gesture,
Whose dusk will come like tact, like a change in the conversation,
Violet and indigo, with strings of lemon streetlamps
Casting their pools into the pools of rain
As the notes of the piano are cast from the top-floor window
Into the square that is always Sunday afternoon.

Money

I am your master and your master's master,
I am the dragon's teeth which you have sown
In the field of dead men's and of live men's bones.

I am the moving belt you cannot turn from:
The threat behind the smiling of the clock:
The paper on which your days are signed and witnessed
Which only the mouse and the moth and the flame dare devour.
I am the rustle of banknotes in your graves,
The crackle of lawyers' seals beneath your tombstones,
Borne to the leaning ears of legatees.

I am the cunning one whose final cunning
Was to buy grace, to corner loveliness,
To make a bid for beauty and to win it
And lock it away.

Advertising

You, without gleam or glint or fire,
You cannot know your own desire.
But I will tell you. I will look through your eyes. Now
    listen!
Here are the toys that please, the almost-gems that glisten! ...
I am your wish and I its answer.
I am the drum and you the dancer.
I am the trumpet-voice, the Stentor.
I am temptation, I the Mentor
Who tells you that ten million men have long
Called a stone bread – and can ten million men be wrong?
I am the voice that bids you spend to save and save to spend,
But always spend that wheels may never end
Their turning and by turning let you spend to save
And save to spend, world without end, cradle to grave.

[36]

Hollywood

I am the fairy-tale, the lovely lie, the brighter-than-truth,
The mirror of transformation, the face of youth
Answering the eye of age with 'I
Am You, and cloudier mirrors lie!'

I am Olympus with the last mist rolled away:
Gods-in-your-image moving in a brighter day.
Watch Venus Anadyomene: she will whitely rise
From seas of arc-lights; these are moons
                                    that were her eyes
And sun that was her hair: for this is She,
Helen and Beatrice, Laura, La Belle Dame
                                    Sans Merci!

Dance band

Swim with the stream! Sleep as you swim! Let the wave take you!
However loud they play, my saxophones will never wake you
For they are in your dream and you in theirs;
My beat is in your blood whose pulse it shares;
My drums are in your veins, close as your heart;
Your flanks are moulded by the waves they part;
This stream's the moving shadow of your thigh.
Dance and forget to die, forget to die!

I am New York aware of Africa and something lost:
I am two exiles, Judah and the jungle, Broadway-crossed:
Nostalgia spangled, fear-of-the-dark striped with bright laughter:
Now in a lighted room, defying *Before* and *After*,
That pair who tap on the window-panes and burrow
    through the bone-thin rafter.

[37]

Radio

Here is another dream, another forgetting, another doorway:

Sound, to drown the sting of the rain on the pane and the sough
　　of the wind
And the sound of the sea:
Sound, like feathers, to muffle the sound of silence
And the beat of the heart:

Sound, to go with you, through the valley of the shadow in the
　　dashboard of the shining car:

The comfortable voice of the announcer purring the ruin of kingdoms
The fall of cities and the fall of wickets,
The random dead and the New Year knights:

Sound like a sea to conceal the bone, the broken shell, the broken ship.

Popular press

I am the echoing rock that sends you back
Your own voice grown so bold that with surprise
You murmur, 'Ah, how sensible I am –
The plain bluff man, the enemy of sham –
How sane, how wise!'

I am the mirror where your image moves,
Neat and obedient twin, until one day
It moves before you move; and it is you
Who have to ape its moods and motions, who
Must now obey.

Love speaks to the lover

If you'd have rest, take shelter, fly,
For every echo may be I,
At every crack may crouch my spy.

But if unrest, turn from your mirror,
Turn from your dream, to joy, to terror,
Unlearn old wisdom, learn new error.

Stand in your thin skin in my sun
Till skin bears fire and bone's immune
Or skin unflakes and bones melt, run.

Unleash, unfurl. Be sail for wind.
Be seed for prodigal hand to spend.
Cease to plan and begin to be planned.

Be loosed, be used: and I the user.
Be called, be chosen: I the chooser.
Or be refused: I the refuser.

Be pricked by spears, be driven by whips,
Be tortured by doubt's water-drips,
and find strange words upon your lips.

Then, when you've left your harbour-ease
For this light raft wind-caught on these
Unsounded and inconstant seas ...

Seek, without chart, Hesperides!

The psychiatrist's song

Learn to know the mind-behind-
Mind that sees when you are blind.
Learn to trust the mind-below-
Mind that's wiser than you know.

Learn to meet the fear you fear,
Hate you hate, and see them clear.
Enter the forbidden place.
Face at last your other face.

Learn to be alone; then only
Reach out hand no longer lonely.
Grow, be tall yet reconciled
To yourself the weeping child.

Love; be easy, and be warm.
Find the fire beyond the form.
Laugh. Forgive yourself; forgive
Sins long dead, and learn to live.

The intellectuals

We invite you into a region
High and with air so thin
That few can breathe such air, but these,
Freed from the burden of gravitation,
Sit upon clouds.

There words are pieces in a game of chess,
And thought is drawn out slender as a long elastic thread,
And systems fit into systems like a nest of tables.

There you can spin like a spider, undisturbed.
There you are free with the freedom of dreams in which
you fly.

The prostitute

I am whom you seek, I am what you want to see,
Any one or no-one, a mirror or an empty face
Or many faces, being as you choose and use me.

I am wife and sister; mistress, mother and daughter;
To one, the one he has sought and never found;
To one, the one he found and changed and hated.

Pour in me like a glass what wine you need,
Write on me like a page what words you wish,
Think that you drug me, fancy you despise me,

But you are the one despised and I have drugged you
And when you wake you will remember nothing
But a little warmth and a hollow in a creaking bed.

The occultist

Come up the narrow stair to the fourth-floor room
And I will show you mystery freed of doom,
Initiation without ordeal, religion rid of anguish of mind,
The magic you cannot find
In your typist's day, at the Woolworth counter, in queues for shoes,
In the one-and-ninepennies worshipping Bing as he sings the Blues:
Something you miss
Between the dancehall and the doorstep kiss:
A flicker of half-seen faces,
Incense in empty places,
Light for the eyes that neon lighting tires,
Smoky fires,
Something you cannot squeeze
Between opening time and finish-your-drinks-up-please,
And find, perhaps, in dreambook revelations
And Moon in Cancer and auras and emanations,
In this magic of half-belief and wonder, in this
Quick brush with bliss.

Smart-boy

I am the Lad: the wide-awake, the smart-boy,
The one who knows the ropes and where he's going,
The easy smiler with the easy money.

I was the kid who got no praise or prizes
Who's now the man to get the peachbloom lovelies:
Black Market Boy with my good mixer manner.

I'm your tall talker in the fug of bar-rooms,
Quick at a deal, an old hand on the dog tracks,
Knowing in clubs, stander at Soho corners.

Go-between guy, I'm wiser than to work for
What the world hands me on a shiny salver,
Me the can't-catch-me-dozing razor-sharp-boy

Ready to set my toe to Order's backside:
Big-shot-to-be, big-city up-and-comer:
Quickstepper, racer, ace among you sleepers.

The lesser artists

We speak to a few of you now, but to many later,
And more still after both you and we have gone,
And we, through you, have left our devious traces:
Ciphers in caves or under a marked stone waiting
For a finder one day to decode, and show to his friends.

We have dealt too much in ciphers; sat in corners,
Out of the wind, talking in undertones
With private signs, drawing too close together,
Drawing the blind.
                        And we have hated the others,
Those behind other blinds.
                        We have been embittered
Too easily by our audience, by the stalls
Staying too long in the bar at intervals,
Yawning behind their hands, and by the gallery's
Catcalls and whistles, crude but half-deserved.

We are the disembowellers who have used
Our own guts and our friends' for strings for fiddles.
We are the eyes and ears at our own keyholes;
The spies on our own whispered conversations;
The ghostly watchers of our copulations,
The third in the narrow bed.
We are that ill-assorted, arrogant, petty,
Incompetent-at-living, glib-at-comment,
Destructive, self-destructive, self-divided,
Restless, rootless, faithless, faith-demanding,
Unsatisfied, unsatisfiable crew
Whom the ironical gods in a casual moment
Chose for their gift of tongues and touched with fire.

The British

We are a people living in shells and moving
Crablike; reticent, awkward, deeply suspicious;
Watching the world from a corner of half-closed eyelids,
Afraid lest someone show that he hates or loves us,
Afraid lest someone weep in the railway train.

We are coiled and clenched like a fœtus clad in armour.
We hold our hearts for fear they fly like eagles.
We grasp our tongues for fear they cry like trumpets.
We listen to our own footsteps. We look both ways
Before we cross the silent empty road.

We are a people easily made uneasy,
Especially wary of praise, of passion, of scarlet
Cloaks, of gesturing hands, of the smiling stranger
In the alien hat who talks to all or the other
In the unfamiliar coat who talks to none.

We are afraid of too-cold thought or too-hot
Blood, of the opening of long-shut shafts or cupboards,
Of light in caves, of X-rays, probes, unclothing
Of emotion, intolerable revelation
Of lust in the light, of love in the palm of the hand.

We are afraid of, one day on a sunny morning,
Meeting ourselves or another without the usual
Outer sheath, the comfortable conversation,
And saying all, all, all we did not mean to,
All, all, all we did not know we meant.

[45]

The neurotics

We are the double people, gaoled and gaoler,
Sparrow and hawk in one uneasy body;
We are a battlefield but cannot clearly
Remember why the fight or when it started.

We are the builders of small doorless houses,
Walls to defy the other world which always
Peers in at us through widening cracks that vainly
We cram with mud or paper or our fingers.

Some of us build our secret world by gathering
Fans or old playing cards or Balkan watches
To hoard and pattern, love and list and label:
Kingdom in which we're king and none may enter.

Some of us build our world with pornographic
Postcards or drugs or mistresses or money,
Private religions or a cipher diary
Or great inventions in an attic drawer.

Some of us spend our lives preventing others
From doing what we cannot or we dare not,
And stand in shadow spitting at the sunlight,
And watch at keyholes for the Day of Judgment.

Some of us play at games with blood and nightmares,
Pricking a tender nerve with mental needles,
Twisting a mind as schoolboys twist a forearm,
Pinning the human fly beneath the tumbler.

Some of us populate our days and nights with
Enemies laying plots to trip or maim us,
To make us halt by roofs when tiles are falling
Or lose umbrellas, chances, buses, lovers.

Some of us wander reaching, reaching, reaching
Backwards in time as down into dark water
To find the clockwork mouse that broke, the woolly
Bear that we lost among the tall black fir-trees.

We are the dwellers in the middle limbo,
Land that we hate yet land that holds our landmarks,
Land where we cannot rest yet stay unresting,
Land that we long to leave but fear to start from.

We are the walkers in eternal circles
To whom the circle's better than its breaking,
To whom unhappiness has long grown easier
Than happiness; to whom this twilight's home.

Epilogue

I am proud, humble, stupid, clever, anonymous
Man, who am lost in the only world I know;
Blind in my mask and tripped by my disguises;
Used by my tools and wounded by my weapons;
Chased by my echo, scared by my long shadow;
Fumbling with delicate hands; longing to be
Myself (who who? but who? if I only knew!);
Groping; self-torn, self-tortured, self-condemned;
Wormeaten angel, welter of dust and flame.

Daydream

One day people will touch and talk perhaps easily,
And loving be natural as breathing and warm as sunlight,
And people will untie themselves, as string is unknotted,
Unfold and yawn and stretch and spread their fingers,
Unfurl, uncurl like seaweed returned to the sea,
And work will be simple and swift as a seagull flying,
And play will be casual and quiet as a seagull settling,
And the clocks will stop, and no-one will wonder
    or care or notice,
And people will smile without reason, even in the winter,
    even in the rain.

The unwept waste

Let funeral marches play,
Let heartbreak-music sound
For the half-death, not the whole;
For the unperceived slow soiling;
For the sleeping before evening;
For what, but for a breath,
But for an inch one way,
The shifting of a scene,
A closed or opened door,
A word less, a word more,
Might have, so simply, been.

The final tragedies are,
Not the bright light dashed out,
Not the gold glory smashed
Like a lamp upon the floor,
But the guttering away,
The seep, the gradual grey,
The unnoticed, without-haste-
Or-protest, premature,
Unwept, unwritten waste.

Not love perhaps

This is not Love perhaps – Love that lays down
Its life, that many waters cannot quench, nor the floods drown –
But something written in lighter ink, said in a lower tone:
Something perhaps especially our own:
A need at times to be together and talk –
And then the finding we can walk
More firmly through dark narrow places
And meet more easily nightmare faces:
A need to reach out sometimes hand to hand –
And then find Earth less like an alien land:
A need for alliance to defeat
The whisperers at the corner of the street:
A need for inns on roads, islands in seas, halts for discoveries
    to be shared,
Maps checked and notes compared:
A need at times of each for each
Direct as the need of throat and tongue for speech.

If men were not striped like tigers

How much simpler if men were not striped like tigers,
    patched like clowns;
If alternate white and black were not further confused
    by greys and browns;
If people were, even at times, consistent wholes;
If the actors were rigidly typed and kept their roles;
If we were able
To classify friends, each with his label,
Each label neat
As the names of cakes or the categories of meat.
But you, my dear, are a greedy bitch, yet also a sad child lost,
And you who have swindled your partners are kind to the cat,
And, in human beings, this is not this nor that quite that
And the threads are crossed
And nothing's as tidy as the mind could wish
And the human mammal is partly insect and often reptile
    and also fish.

England

(Autumn 1938)

Plush bees above a bed of dahlias;
  Leisurely, timeless garden teas;
Brown bread and honey; scent of mowing;
  The still green light below tall trees.

    The ancient custom of deception;
      A Press that seldom stoops to lies –
    Merely suppresses truth and twists it,
      Blandly corrupt and slyly wise.

The Common Man; his mask of laughter;
  His back-chat while the roof falls in;
Minorities' long losing battles
  Fought that the sons of sons may win.

    The politicians' inward snigger
      (Big Business on the private phone);
    The knack of sitting snug on fences;
      The double face of flesh and stone.

Grape-bloom of distant woods at dusk;
  Storm-crown on Glaramara's head;
The fire-rose over London night;
  An old plough rusting autumn-red.

    The 'incorruptible policeman'
      Gaoling the whore whose bribe's run out,
    Guarding the rich against the poor man,
      Guarding the Settled Gods from doubt.

The generous smile of music-halls,
  Bars and bank-holidays and queues;
The private peace of public foes;
  The truce of pipe and football news.

The smile of privilege exultant;
  Smile at the 'bloody Red' defeated;
Smile at the striker starved and broken;
  Smile at the 'dirty nigger' cheated.

The old hereditary craftsman;
  The incommunicable skill;
The pride in long-loved tools, refusal
  To do the set job quick or ill.

    The greater artist mocked, misflattered;
      The lesser forming clique and team
    Or crouching in his narrow corner,
      Narcissus with his secret dream.

England of rebels – Blake and Shelley;
  England where freedom's sometimes won,
Where Jew and Negro needn't fear yet
  Lynch-law and pogrom, whip and gun.

    England of cant and smug discretion;
      England of wagecut-sweatshop-knight,
    Of sportsman-churchman-slum-exploiter,
      Of puritan grown sour with spite.

England of clever fool, mad genius,
  Timorous lion and arrogant sheep,
Half-hearted snob and shamefaced bully,
  Of hands that wake and eyes that sleep ...
England the snail that's shod with lightning ...
  Shall we laugh or shall we weep?

Where?

You are in love with a country
Where people laugh in the sun
And the people are warm as the sunshine and live and move easily
And women with honeycoloured skins and men with no
    frowns on their faces
Sit on white terraces drinking red wine
While the sea spreads peacock feathers on cinnamon sands
And palms weave sunlight into sheaves of gold
And at night the shadows are indigo velvet
And there is dancing to soft, soft, soft guitars
Played by copper fingers under a froth of stars.

Perhaps your country is where you think you will find it.
Or perhaps it has not yet come or perhaps it has gone.
Perhaps it is east of the sun and west of the moon.
Perhaps it is a country called the Hesperides
And Avalon and Atlantis and Eldorado:
A country which Gauguin looked for in Tahiti and
    Lawrence in Mexico,
And whether they found it only they can say, and they not now.
Perhaps you will find it where you alone can see it,
But if you can see it, though no one else can, it will be there,
It will be yours.

Saving grace

Fish do not smile, nor birds: their faces are not
Equipped for it. A smiling dog's the illusion
And wish-fulfilment of its owner. Cats wear
Permanent smiles inspired by mere politeness.
But human animals at times forget their
Godlike responsibilities; the tension
Slackens, the weasel-sharp intentness falters;
Muscles relax; the eyes refrain from peering
Aside, before and after; and the burden
Of detail drops from forehead; cheekline gently
Creases; the mouth wide-flowers; the stiff mask softens;
And Man bestows his simple, unambitious,
Unservile, unselfseeking, undeceptive,
Uncorrupt gift, the grace-note of a smile.

Jigsaw

This one can understand but cannot act,
Defeated by detachment and division.
That one can act but cannot understand,
Defeated by desire and concentration.
This one can gain and grasp but not enjoy,
Defeated by his haste and heat and hardness;
And that one can enjoy but not acquire,
Defeated by his softness and self-loving.
And so the half-man seeks the one he is not,
The friend or lover moving where he cannot,
The other terminal, the arc's completion,
The periscope with which to see round corners,
The one who still may someday, somewhere, somehow
Lead him across the frontiers of forbidden
Land, to a world reversed, looking-glass country
Beyond this bondage and beyond this boredom
Of this too known, too own world, this round narrow
Room here behind the mouth and nose and eyes.

Horoscope for Diane

Born beneath a troubled star,
Lovelier than others are,
Brighter with the flame of life,
You will cause and suffer strife.

Where you go there will be war;
Where you walk, will walk before
Flattery, and at your back
Envy waiting to attack.

When you look for friends you'll find
Would-be lovers, hungry, blind;
Whom you think you touch and pass,
See! behind you in your glass:

You to whom fate gave the unwise,
Irremediable prize,
Beauty burning, doomed to fire
Too much undesired desire.

Talk in the night

'Why are you sighing?'
     'For all the voyages I did not make
     Because the boat was small, might leak, might take
     The wrong course, and the compass might be broken,
     And I might have awoken
     In some strange sea and heard
     Strange birds crying.'

'Why are you weeping?'
     'For all the unknown friends or lovers passed
     Because I watched the ground or walked too fast
     Or simply did not see
     Or turned aside for tea
     For fear an old wound stirred
     From its sleeping.'

The same hour will not strike

          'Nothing happens twice,
          And the same rain will not fall,
          And the same wind will not pass,'
          Said the Lover sadly, sadly,
             Looking at the girl
                Looking in the glass.

          'Nothing happens twice,
          And the same rain will not fall,
          And the same stream will not run,'
          Said the Lost One gladly, gladly,
             Groping past the Horror,
                Past the Shadow, to the Sun.

The old witch said

'To-day,' the old witch bending over the cradle said,
'A web is weaving that won't be finished until you're dead.

And you who think you are free will find that threads are round you
And those you love and those who love you, child, have bound you.

'And you who think you escape, my child, will find you arrive at
The place you run from, meet the face you avoid, connive at

'The crime you hate, remember words in the book you're burning.
And everywhere are ripples turning and returning.

'And when you move an arm in the dark you'll touch a shoulder;
And when you move a foot you'll stir a sliding boulder.

'And even your grave will raise entangling hands for a while,
As I, the witch, the weaver, unravel the threads, and smile.'

Split world

Too many books
 Are written, read
By those who live
 Within the head
And word-born words
 Are interbred;

And books are read
 By those who write,
And dog eats dog,
 And light and light –
Conflicting, crossed –
 Confuse the sight;

And one can think,
 Another do,
But messages
 Come rarely through
Deserts that lie
 Between the two.

Conversation for three

Says Mind, 'Can you love her, Heart, can you love her still,
Knowing how many seemed lovely once and how many will?'
Says Blood, 'Can you love her more than your lust, Heart, more
Than the warmth, the blindness, the flight from questions, the rest from war?'
Says Mind, 'Can you love her more than you love the chase,
Through my intricate mirror-maze, of your own quick-changing face?
Can you love as simply as sleeping or holding a hand
Yet as boldly as taking a path to an unknown land?
Can you love through time's long rain and hail and thunder
With me on the watch above and round and under?
Heart, can you love her as much as yourself, I wonder?'
                And Heart repeats
'Yes,' to the Mind and the Blood, to the two slick tyrannous cheats.

Acknowledgement

When I was lonely
Your fingers reached for mine, their touch
Natural as sunlight's.

When I was hardened
Your warmness thawed my rock as gently
As music thought.

When I was angry
You smiled: 'But this our day is short
For these long shadows.'

When I was solemn
You held out laughter, casual as light
For a cigarette.

When I was troubled
Your understanding crossed the bounds of
Words to silence.

When I was frightened
Your eyes said: 'Fear's a child's dream. I too
Have dreamed and woken.'

Song

A year ago, I was saying,
'I must be free as air
To turn at any street-corner
And stop on any stair
And follow the shadow of any eyelash,
The flare of passing hair.'

To-day, I find myself saying,
'I need north-south; a pole;
Lodestone and fixed abode, now;
Compass; a map; control;
Something less cold than the fugitive eye;
Not part of love, but the whole.'

Is it the end of youth, then
(Youth not young unless wild)?
Or is it the slow beginning
Of ceasing to be a child
Playing with bricks or the sun in water;
Half-born, self-beguiled?

After attempted escape from love

He who has once been caught in a silver chain may burn
and toss and fret.
He will never be bound with bronze again; he will not
be forgiven; will never forget.
He who has eaten the golden grapes of the sun will call
no sour fruit sweet.
He will turn from the moon's green apples and run,
though they fall in his hand, though they lie at his
feet.

Postscript to a pettiness

Though you'll forgive (I think, my sweet)
My larger sins of haste and heat
And lust and fear, can you forgive
My inabilities to live?
Can you despise me not too much
When most I lack the human touch,
And keep no date, no diary of
Days when I fail, dear love, to love?

Footnotes on happiness

Happiness filters
Out through a crack in the door, through the net's reticulations.
But also in.

The old cat Patience
Watching the hole with folded paws and quiet tail
Can seldom catch it.

Timetables fail.
It rarely stands at a certain moment a certain day
At a certain bus-stop.

You cannot say
It will keep an appointment, or pass the same street corner twice.
Nor say it won't.

Lavender, ice,
Camphor, glass cases, vacuum chambers hermetically sealed,
Won't keep it fresh.

It will not yield
Except to the light, the careless, the accidental hand,
And easily bruises.

It is brittle as sand.
It is more and less than you hoped to find. It has never quite
Your own ideas.

It shows no spite
Or favour in choosing its host. It is, like God,
Casual, odd.

Invitation to the dance

Enough, my brain, of these circles, circles.
  Cease, caged enemy, cease.
Others have thought these thoughts before you.
  Peace, brain; peace.

It has all been written in books, and better.
  Come; let the tidal sweep
Of the music run through our veins' slow delta.
  (Sleep, brain; sleep.)

Music will rise in us, rise like the dance of
  Growth; like sap's long riot.
Limbs understand. Thighs have their language.
  (Quiet, brain; quiet.)

Listen. This tune is a sea, resolving
  Crest upon breaking crest.
Feet weave a web that unweaves behind us.
  Rest, brain; rest. Rest.

Money talks

Money talks with a voice that's thinned
To a rustle of chequebooks in the wind.

Money talks with a voice as dry
As an auditor's enquiring eye.

Money talks with a voice that clanks
Like slamming doors of closing banks.

Money talks with the hollow sound
Of metal boxes underground.

'Inflation's floods are dark and drear.
The deserts of deflation sear.

My enemies are always near.'
Money talks with a voice of fear.

Deaf animal

Man can talk, but seldom
Listen; for he hears
Less the words that are spoken
Than his own hopes and fears.

Man can be taught perhaps only
That which he almost knows
For only in soil that is ready
Grows the mind's obstinate rose.

The right word at the wrong time
Is wind-caught, blown away;
And the most that the ages' sages'
Wisdom and wit can say

Is no more to the quickest pupil
Than a midwife's delicate steady
Fingers aiding and easing
The thought half-born already.

And argument is either
A game light as a smile
Where each side's equal cheating
Observes the laws of guile,

Or a bitter and bleeding duel
Fought by the angry and blind
(But tomorrow the loser will vanquish
The victor's ghost in his mind).

And all the comforter's eager
Awkward speech is only
A song-without-words whose tune will
Lull, perhaps, the lonely.

The firewalkers

They give themselves without stint
To joy and sorrow and taint,
To love and life and desire;
They walk in the noon, in the fire;
They scorch but they do not tire;
They fall but they do not faint.

They are not closed or cold,
Furled, folded away or old;
They do not refuse or withhold;
They have never stayed to rest;
They have slept where they have stood;
And few will call them good,
But some will call them blest.

The lesson

'There's nothing,' you said, 'that's worth regretting
  Save what one has not done,
Not dared, not taken, not tried, not trusted:
  One's turnings from the sun.'

'Not many,' you said, 'can catch at morning
  The quick bird Now; but oh
Fewer, still fewer, can let him at evening
  Easily, lightly go.'

'You, I,' you said, 'we are each of us many,
  And each of the many must say
To the others, "Unknown, I disown you: here's only
  I, and this, my day."'

To a girl who would like to be a cynic

Sentimentalist who'd die
Rather than admit you're one,
Flying from yourself you run
Fast – so fast that one day I
Think you'll turn a corner, start,
Stand and – come full circle – meet
Your accusing exiled heart
Triumphing in your defeat.
And the tears that would not rise
Into your resistant eyes,
All the too-long-waiting tears,
All the prides and all the fears,
All at last will fall, and all
Loose you, free you as they fall!

Masque of all men

In the cold-windy cavern of the Wings
With skeletons of unused sets above them
The actors' painted heads clustered,
Clustered and whispered. One head whispered,
'This has been my life: the Prologue often,
And then no Play. Or when the play has come
The players have departed, the parts being played
By understudies, makeshifts, shifting
The balance, the play, the purpose:
The lines dissolving and the play transposing
Itself into another, an unrehearsed;
So that the prompter, script discarded, idly
Sits in the echoing cavern
Among cold winds beneath the unused sets.'

And others whispered, 'Your life? Yes, and mine.'
'And mine.' 'And mine.' 'And mine.'
                                        'And mine.'
                                        'And mine.'

Whisper of a thin ghost

I bought the books of the Careful-Wise
And I read the rules in a room apart
And I learned to clothe my flinching heart
Against hate and love and inquisitive eyes
In the Coat of Caution, the Shirt of Pride.
And then, the day before I died,
I found that the rules of the wise had lied:
That life was a blood-warm stream that ran
Through the fields of death, and that no man can
Bathe in the stream but the naked man.
And that is why my ghost now must
So grope, so grieve, as grieve all those
In whom death found no wounds to close,
In whom dust found no more than dust.

Rock-edge

Some of the finest people I have known,
The few, the fine who keep their sun at noon,
The unrefusing, the warmly living and giving,
Too gaily walk on a razor-edge of mountain
From which a sudden gust from a certain quarter
Could topple them down to darkness and destruction.
No one can save them from themselves or chance.
World, move gently
Your clumsy finger lest
So much be spoiled and lost.

Paris café, 1938

A far accordion gaily grieves.
Sunlight slants through roofs of leaves
Into green or golden glass.
Public lovers smiling pass.
Short square women dressed in black
Talk for ever. Waiters stack
Saucers. Ice clinks. Colours shake,
Heat-stirred. White walls bake and flake.

Fate writes two epitaphs

I
On any man

I let him find, but never what he sought;
I let him act, but never as he meant;
And, after much mislearning, he was taught,
Tired, to be content with discontent.

II
On man

He had great virtues, but a seed of terror
Corrupted him; fear made him cruel, mean;
So I repealed an all-but glorious error,
Wiped off a little dust, and left earth clean.

Sleep: I

The ring and rim
Of tidal sleep
Wiil slip and creep
Along my limbs

And I shall watch,
But never catch
The final change,
The water-plunge,

And through what caves
Beneath what waves
I then shall go
I shall not know

For I shall come
From that lost land
Half-blind, half-dumb,
With, in my hand,

A fish's head,
A shell, a shred
Of seaweed and
Some grains of sand.

Age

Do men grow wholly old;
Unknowing, tire of living;
Grow deaf as pulse grows faint;
Dream and in dreams depart?

Or do they wake, feel cold
And hear – a salt sea grieving
In landlocked, long complaint –
The all-too-youthful heart?

Poems first collected in *Selection*

Portrait of a romantic

He is in love with the land that is always over
The next hill and the next, with the bird that is never
Caught, with the room beyond the looking-glass.

He likes the half-hid, the half-heard, the half-lit,
The man in the fog, the road without an ending,
Stray pieces of torn words to piece together.

He is well aware that man is always lonely,
Listening for an echo of his cry, crying for the moon,
Making the moon his mirror, weeping in the night.

He often dives in the deep-sea undertow
Of the dark and dreaming mind. He turns at corners,
Twists on his heel to trap his following shadow.

He is haunted by the face behind the face.
He searches for last frontiers and lost doors.
He tries to climb the wall around the world.

Middle-aged conversation

'Are you sad to think how often
    You have let all wisdom go
For a crimson mouth and rounded
    Thighs and eyes you drowned in?' 'No.'

'Do you find this level country,
    Where the winds more gently blow,
Better than the summit raptures
    And the deep-sea sorrows?' 'No.'

Black Monday lovesong

In love's dances, in love's dances
One retreats and one advances.
One grows warmer and one colder,
One more hesitant, one bolder.
One gives what the other needed
Once, or will need, now unheeded.
One is clenched, compact, ingrowing
While the other's melting, flowing.
One is smiling and concealing
While the other's asking, kneeling.
One is arguing or sleeping
While the other's weeping, weeping.

And the question finds no answer
And the tune misleads the dancer
And the lost look finds no other
And the lost hand finds no brother
And the word is left unspoken
Till the theme and thread are broken.

When shall these divisions alter?
Echo's answer seems to falter:
'Oh the unperplexed, unvexed time
Next time ... one day ... one day ... next time!'

A hot day

Cottonwool clouds loiter.
A lawnmower, very far,
Birrs. Then a bee comes
To a crimson rose and softly,
Deftly and fatly crams
A velvet body in.

A tree, June-lazy, makes
A tent of dim green light.
Sunlight weaves in the leaves,
Honey-light laced with leaf-light,
Green interleaved with gold.
Sunlight gathers its rays
In sheaves, which the wind unweaves
And then reweaves – the wind
That puffs a smell of grass
Through the heat-heavy, trembling
Summer pool of air.

Skaters' Waltz

... So tempting to let freeze
  One's deepest, darkest pools
And learn to skim with ease
  Thin ice; for who but fools

Dive into who-knows-what?'
  'But if the ice by chance
Breaks?' 'But if not, if not?
  And how it glitters! Dance!'

Jamaican bus ride

The live fowl squatting on the grapefruit and bananas
in the basket of the copper-coloured lady
is gloomy but resigned.
The four very large baskets on the floor
are in everybody's way,
as the conductor points out
loudly, often, but in vain.

Two quadroon dandies are disputing
who is standing on whose feet.

When we stop,
a boy vanishes through the door marked ENTRANCE;
but those entering through the door marked EXIT
are greatly hindered by the fact that when we started
there were twenty standing,
and another ten have somehow inserted themselves
into invisible crannies
between dark sweating body and body.

With an odour of petrol
both excessive and alarming
we hurtle hell-for-leather
between crimson bougainvillaea blossom
and scarlet poinsettia
and miraculously do not run over
three goats, seven hens and a donkey
as we pray
that the driver has not fortified himself
at Daisy's Drinking Saloon
with more than four rums:
or by the gods of Jamaica
this day is our last!

A man of culture

He finds that talk of music, books and art is
Useful at all the most important parties.
He cultivates an aptitude for knowing
Which way the day's aesthetic wind is blowing.
He lacks all passion, feels no love or hate;
Notes what is up to, what is out of, date;
Is equally prepared to praise or damn
So long as he can coin an epigram.
Spying the coming man before he's come,
He beats the first premonitory drum;
Aware which reputation's almost dead,
He plans the funeral speech a year ahead.
His seismographic needle will betray
A falling fashion half the world away;
Yet good and bad in art are one to him,
Mirror of mode and weathercock of whim.

Established in his eminence of taste,
This little man has little time to waste:
And so the only books at which he looks
Are books on books, or books on books on books.
He shines, but shines with cold reflected light,
Bold without risk, derivatively right,
Lame but for crutches, but for prompters dumb,
Index of others, every summary's sum,
Rich by much robbing, smart at second hand,
Builder with borrowed bricks on shifting sand,
Reaper of fields dug deep by earlier spades,
Echo of echoes, shadower of shades.

The psycho-analyst

His suit is good, his hands are white.
He smiles all day and sleeps all night
Because he's always, always right.

He states his theory. You agree?
Well then, of course, it's plain to see
That he is right as right can be!

You disagree? Ah, that is mere
Resistance to the facts you fear:
Truth is confirmed, the case is clear!

So you are free as air to choose,
Take his advice or spurn his views,
But heads he wins and tails you lose.

His fees are large, his cares are light,
His analytic eyes are bright,
He glows with pride as well he might.

The analyst is always right.

She

No more time or place
Once I see her face.
Sorrow, doubt and fear
Leave when she is near.
Warm, her eyes and hand,
Wordless, understand.

She, although away,
Stays with me all day,
In, below, behind
Blood and heart and mind.
She is where I go.
She is all I know.

Goal and map: to her
I relate, refer
All experience,
Feeling, thought and sense.
Each discovery
Is a prize to be

Shown to her one day:
Something I can lay
Proud before her feet:
Something to repeat:
New-discovered door
We may find once more.

Every day's begun
Charted by her sun.
All I shall not share
Who-knows-when-or-where
With her, and re-taste
By her side, is waste.

The advisers

Reason says, 'Love a girl who does not love you?
  Learn to forget her, learn to let her go!'
But Fate says, 'When I sent you far to find her
  I had a plan whose end you cannot know.'

Reason says, 'Love like this will bring you a thousand
  Unhappy days for every happy hour.'
'To give great joy,' says Fate, 'without great suffering,
  Light without shadow, lies beyond my power.'

'Can you,' says Reason, 'love a girl in love with
  Another man? Have you no pride, no will?'
'I am using you,' says Fate; 'have faith; be humble.
  Tools are not told what purpose they fulfil.'

'What she needs,' Reason says, 'you cannot give her,
  Nor she what you need.' 'No, not now,' says Fate;
'But both of you will change. When you are ready
  To play your parts, you will. Be patient. Wait.'

Reason says, 'If you chase a dream through darkness,
  What but confusion, misery can you find?'
Fate says, 'Before you lies a long hard journey,
  But I can see the way though you are blind.'

Reason says, 'Look, there are easier paths to choose from
  And lesser goals with greater hopes of gain.'
But Fate says, 'You are the chosen, not the chooser.
  I give you, friend, the privilege of pain.'

Conversation with myself

'Lie down, heart. Do not run to meet her. See,
The path is clear and who can come but she?
Rest now, let be.
When two, as you and she, agree
To laugh at time, they're timeless, free.
Let go. Let be.

Let be; here's none but you and she and fate.
Your world's without dimension, distance, date;
And all things come, fool heart, to those who wait.'
'No, no. Love has dimension, distance, date;
And all things come perhaps to those who wait ...
But some too late.'

Lovers' conversation

'Why do we hurt each other,
    We two, so much and often?
Why does the heart so quickly
    Harden and slowly soften?'

'Love itself hurts the lover
    Who sighs and cries for release
From the joy that is partly sorrow
    And the passion that's never peace.'

Two men in a dance hall

Tom laughs, is free and easy;
   And girls obey his call,
For whether they obey it
   He hardly cares at all.

But Edward burns with longing;
   And angry anxious pain
Cries from his eyes too loudly,
   Too eagerly, in vain.

The implacable streets

On certain afternoons
The streets start to repeat
Themselves and after the corner
The faces at the windows
Are the same and the gulf between
The walls is very tall
And houses suddenly lean
Closer and there's no clue
And everyone you meet
Is lost without retreat
And each one hunts in vain
For an unknown address
And all begins again.

Poems first collected in
Not love perhaps ...

The too much loved

It has been written in your star
That fire shall kindle where you are:
That where you walk there shall be strife;
Ice melting; earth turned; sleep stirred; life.

You will graze hearts and blood will spurt,
You will be hurt because you hurt
Those whom you try not even to touch,
Whose eyes pursue your eyes too much.

You will bring peace but oftener still
Wars in your name against your will;
Yet you divider, waker of
Angers will suffer too much love.

And you will stir the whirlpool up,
And you will drink the unasked for cup,
And be of those much damned and blessed
Who never rest, who never rest.

The ad-man

This trumpeter of nothingness, employed
To keep our reason full and null and void:
This man of wind and froth and flux will sell
The wares of any who reward him well,
Praising whatever he is paid to praise,
He hunts for ever-newer, smarter ways
To make the gilt seem gold; the shoddy, silk;
To cheat us legally; to bluff and bilk
By methods which no jury can prevent
Because the law's not broken, only bent.

This mind for hire, this mental prostitute
Can tell the half-lie hardest to refute;
Knows how to hide an inconvenient fact
And when to leave a doubtful claim unbacked;
Manipulates the truth, but not too much,
And if his patter needs the Human Touch
Then aptly artless, artfully naive,
He wears his fickle heart upon his sleeve.

He takes ideas and trains them to engage
In the long little wars big combines wage.
He keeps his logic loose, his feelings flimsy;
Turns eloquence to cant and wit to whimsy;
Trims language till it fits his client's pattern,
And style's a glossy tart or limping slattern.

He uses words that once were strong and fine.
Primal as sun and moon and bread and wine,
True, honourable, honoured, clear and clean,
And leaves them shabby, worn, diminished, mean.

Where our defence is weakest, he attacks.
Encircling reason's fort, he finds the cracks,
He knows the hopes and fears on which to play.
We who at first rebel, at last obey.
We who have tried to choose accept his choice.
Tired, we succumb to his untiring voice.
The drip-drip-drip makes even granite soften.
We trust the brand-name we have heard so often,
And join the queue of sheep that flock to buy:
We fools who know our folly, you and I.

The bargain

Love hurt you once, you said, too much.
You said you'd have no more of such
Hot heartbreak and long loneliness.
You said you'd give and ask for less
Than love, that daemon without pity,
That far, miraged, red, golden city
Across the desert of desire,
Ringed with the gateless ring of fire.

You said you'd drink, but not too deep,
Of life: explore yet always keep
Your final secret self intact,
Entire, untied, untorn, unracked.

And I, may heaven forgive me, said,
'Lay your blonde beloved head
In the hollow of my arm:
We'll love lightly without harm
To either's heart; and I'll defy
Your warmth and loveliness; and I
Won't love too much'.

       Forgive my lie!

Heaven

In the heaven of the god I hope for (call him X)
There is marriage and giving in marriage and transient sex
For those who will cast the body's vest aside
Soon, but are not yet wholly rarefied
And still embrace. For X is never annoyed
Or shocked; has read his Jung and knows his Freud,
He gives you time in heaven to do as you please,
To climb love's gradual ladder by slow degrees,
Gently to rise from sense to soul, to ascend
To a world of timeless joy, world without end.

Here on the gates of pearl there hangs no sign
Limiting cakes and ale, forbidding wine.
No weakness here is hidden, no vice unknown.
Sin is a sickness to be cured, outgrown.
With the help of a god who can laugh, an unsolemn god
Who smiles at old wives' tales of iron rod
And fiery hell, a god who's more at ease
With bawds and Falstaffs than with pharisees.

Here the lame learn to leap, the blind to see.
Tyrants are taught to be humble, slaves to be free.
Fools become wise, and wise men cease to be bores,
Here bishops learn from lips of back-street whores,
And white men follow black-faced angels' feet
Through fields of orient and immortal wheat.

Villon, Lautrec and Baudelaire are here.
Here Swift forgets his anger, Poe his fear.
Napoleon rests. Columbus, journey done,
Has reached his new Atlantis, found his sun.
Verlaine and Dylan Thomas drink together.
Marx talks to Plato. Byron wonders whether
There's some mistake. Wordsworth has found a hill
That's home. Here Chopin plays the piano still.
Wren plans ethereal domes; and Renoir paints
Young girls as ripe as fruit but not yet saints.

And X, of whom no coward is afraid,
Who's friend consulted, not fierce king obeyed;
Who hears the unspoken thought, the prayer unprayed;
Who expects not even the learned to understand
His universe, extends a prodigal hand,
Full of forgiveness, over his promised land.

In Canterbury cathedral

Trees, but straighter than birches, rise to the sky
Of stone. Their branches meet in the sky of stone.
Stone fountains leap and meet: their traceries are
As light as lace. These prayers of stone were prayed
To a God I can't believe in, but were made
By Man, men almost gods, in whom I can
Believe: were made as strong, to last as long
As time. I stare and pray to Man alone.

Master of hypochondria

How happily you sit among a host of
Cures to part-cure the ills you make the most of:
You who are many doctors, many patients
Rolled into one; who plan your permutations
With tranquilliser counteracting tonic,
Stimulant, sedative: Napoleonic
Maestro of civil war: Bach with a theme
As long as life, as lovely as a dream!

Expert in analgesics, trained in taking
Aspirin soon enough to end the aching
Anti-biotics often leave behind them,
You master pains with pains and do not mind them.

Teach me your alchemy! I'll plumb and ponder
Psychosomatic mysteries. I'll wander
Deep in your maze. I'll learn from you to study
My graph, my chart, head neither bowed nor bloody.
We'll meet in Samarkand, the golden city
Of all who play the trumpets of self-pity,
Whose hearts lament like violins above
The thunder-roll of drums men call self-love.

Night-life

The useful and domestic cat
Adorning the familial mat,
Now at the fall of purple dusk,
Suffers a change. He sheds the husk
Of civilisation, and returns
To his primeval self. He burns
With atavistic nomadry,
And yearns to be abroad and free;
Nor longer loves the household lars,
But only seeks the cruel stars ...
Now he is in the pallid gleam
His fur unsleeks, his features seem
To assume a diabolic leer,
His eyes expand, he cocks an ear:
And all the urbanity of day
Turns to an ardent lust for prey ...
But when comes dawn, with slaked desire,
He sits again before the fire.

The psychiatrist speaks

Quietly, patiently I wait
(And sometimes gently probe and peer)
To find the love, the lust, the hate,
The wound, the mystery, the fear
Within the mind-within-the-mind;
The mind that's like a face behind
A window-curtain seeing unseen,
The mind that's wiser than you know,
The mind that says the things you mean,
The mind that's swift when you are slow,
The mind that wakes when daylight mind
Sleeps – and that sees when the other's blind;
The mind that seems to lie so still
But moves calm-surely to its goal
As compass-needle moves to pole.

And then – when I (or rather you)
Have found the last and deepest clue,
The hate you hate, the fear you fear,
The worm that lies beneath the stone,
The ghost in that one room alone
Whose door you never dare unlock,
The secret you've forgotten so
Successfully so long ago
(And yet it's in that ticking clock,
It's on your track behind your back,
Slowly, invisibly drawing near,
Softly preparing to attack) –
Then I say, 'Learn at last to live
Without your sackcloth, to forgive
Yourself the innocent sin, to cast
The burden of guilt away at last!'

Edith Piaf

Voice of one whose heart
   Has mended with the years,
One who can stand apart
   And laugh at life through tears.

Voice of one who has long
   Outlived regret, outgrown
Hope, and at last is strong
   Enough to stand alone.

Summer night at Hyde Park Corner

Great globes of light spill yellow rain:
   Pencils of gold through purple gloom.
The buses swarm like heavy bees
   Trailing fat bodies. Faces loom,
Moonlike, and fade away among the trees
   Which, lit beneath by lamplight, bloom
High in darkness. Distant traffic
   Sounds with dull, enclosing boom ...

Sleep extends a velvet forepaw.
   Night spreads out a downsoft plume.

La marche des machines

(suggested by Deslav's film of the same title)

This piston's infinite recurrence is
night morning night and morning night and
death and birth and death and birth and this
crank climbs (blind Sisyphus) and see

steel teeth greet
bow deliberate
delicately lace
in lethal kiss
        God's teeth bite whitely tight

slowly the gigantic oh slowly the steel spine dislocates

wheels grazing (accurately missing) waltz

two cranes do a hundred-ton tango against the sky.

Poems first collected in
Morning meeting

.

Letter from Luton

Dear Hubert,
              Bored, malevolent and mute on
A wet park seat, I look at life and Luton
And think of spittle, slaughterhouses, double
Pneumonia, schizophrenia, kidney trouble,
Piles, paranoia, gallstones in the bladder,
Manic depressive madness growing madder,
Cretins with hideous tropical diseases
And red-eyed necrophiles – while on the breezes
From Luton Gasworks comes a stench that closes
Like a damp frigid hand on my neuroses;
And Time (arthritic deaf-mute) stumbles on
And on and on and on.
                        Yours glumly,
                              John

The lonely women in hotel lounges

Pity us,
Us the unloved, unlovely and unloving,
Half-loving a cat, our morning tea, jewels in a trunk,
Warmth and a little ease.
Pity our too much peace;
Our absence of release;
Our long days falling without cease;
Us who have missed and still at moments know we miss
Life's bonfire and his kiss.

In a city

How can I apportion
out of this hubbub
room enough to breathe,
space enough to be?
how can I hollow
an invisible cavern
so that I may pause
and, cloistered within it,
recollect all those things
which I am in imminent danger of forgetting,
and renew my contact with things precarious, intangible,
and disentangle all that is obscure,
and consolidate all that is insecure,
and become at any rate something more
than a chance cohesion of moods,
than a mere mechanism of life –
there in that clear vantage ground,
tall tower,
cool recess?

Epitaph on a scoundrel

Shallow, but with so much
    Of tact and grace,
He cheated you with such
    A winning face
That you preferred the charm
    Of hand that hurt you
To the protecting arm
    Of clumsy virtue.

Speech

Clumsily inarticulate
(Inquisitive eyes gaze towards eyes:
Mind gropes down long blind alleys of alien mind)
We try to surprise

Into recognition some strange and isolate being
With legs, arms, hands as ourselves:
Yet cannot touch. Thought's uncontacting vicious
Circle again revolves.

I am dumb, you deaf. I try in vain to fashion
A convention of common speech,
A password. Babel reigns still: each is unable
To understand each ...

Musicians, who weave a thinner web than words' –
Whose clouds but graze the peaks of thought –
Whose perfumes flow in the dark of the mind, – have you found
Some way, have you caught

Some marginal slight inflection, some queer trick
Whereby you can
Make man from his tall tower sometimes speak
To imprisoned man?

Silent cinema

Light you have sung:
light
opalescent, iridescent, wineclouded,
shadowlaced, hyaline;
barred and fenced with darkness,
furred with darkness (velvet
dust-bloom-delicate), light
prismed, imprisoned,
plumed, inwoven

Brittle arpeggios of light;
light long wave upon wave,
pressing our eyelids backwards;
light slow-opening a flower
(fire-rose), light unpetalling,
dusting with flakes of pollen
our upturned
faces

Rondo of light on waves,
scherzo of light on leaves,
light webbed by wings to a wild toccata,
counterpoint – fugue – of light

Birth of light
            slight white
                        breath
                                    blurring dark's mirror

Death of light
            flight
                        as night's
                                    broad slow fans
                                                close

The fishmonger

Sleek through his fingers
the fishes slide,
glisten and curve
and slap their tails
on the smooth white slab ...

silver on marble
ranged they lie.

The fishmonger's hands
are cold with eternal
halibut, haddock,
hake and cod;

his arms are swollen
and red beside
the delicate silver
of the slender fishes;

but his eyes are glazed
and dull like theirs
and his mouth gapes
in codlike wonder

at the flickering stream
that slips through his fingers!

What is this wind

What is this wind that bends
The heavy harvest
Of heads sunk over morning newspapers
On tops of trams and buses? –
That bends the clerk's head over his ledger,
That bows dark heads of women in half-lit churches
(Lonely women congregated in prayer –
Dark corn, a black tide washing up to the altar),
That has bent the reluctant heads of boys and girls
        over lesson-books,
The faded heads of old women in hotel lounges over
        knitting or whispered gossip,
And that blows, a final steel-grey wind,
Bending the stalk straight backwards to the root,
Snapping the brittle stem and leaving it
Withered and only fit
For a pit in the earth?

Romantic

Enfurl the sun in tatters, smoky-red
And black; and in a torn, imperial shroud
Let the sun die as my love dies!
And set a fiery cloud
As background for her unforgiving eyes;
Spill the full winecup of the skies
As mine is spilt! with hell-fire aureole her proud
Head, unlike mine, unbowed!

Sunweb

'Weave, weave the sunlight in your hair' – T. S. Eliot

Sunlight weaves in the corn,
honeylight meshes the honeystalks,
lacing the stems with light
till the net is tight and swings
in the golden wind.

Sunlight weaves in your hair,
sheaving its fiery petals
into your cooler showers,
its hot-gold in their cold-gold,
its hot flowers in their shade.

Sunlight weaves in your eyes,
loosening its leaves and shaking them,
allowing its spears to be broken
by a hundred mirrors and errors;
threshing their pools to ripples;
drowned and found and drowned.

Genius rewarded

He lived ... He hardly could expect us to
    Appreciate assaults upon our habits:
Better those gentlemen who'd bring, we knew,
    From the old hat the old familiar rabbits.

He died ... We said, 'Sir, for your good alone,
    You realise, we threw those brickbats at you?
But now you're dead we feel we should atone.
    Accept – as some slight tribute, sir – this statue!

Autumn

Already men are brushing up
　Brown leaves around the saddened parks.
At Marble Arch the nights draw in
　Upon expounders of Karl Marx.

By the Round Pond the lovers feel
　Heavier dews, and grow uneasy.
Elderly men don overcoats,
　Catch cold – sniff – become hoarse and wheezy.

Grey clouds streak across chill white skies.
　Refuse and dirty papers blow
About the gutters. Shoppers hurry,
　Oppressed by vague autumnal woe.

The cats that pick amongst the empty
　Gold Flake boxes, sniffing orts
From frowsy fish-shops, seem beruffled,
　Limp of tail and out of sorts.

Policemen are pale and *fin-de-siècle*.
　The navvy's arm wilts and relaxes.
With more than usual bitterness
　Bus-drivers curse impulsive taxis.

A general malaise descends:
　Desire for something none can say.
And autumn brings once more the pangs
　Of this our annual decay!

Sunday at home

Having perused at ease *The News of the World*
For juicy titbits of the world's ill-doing –
Murder and rape and richer, cryptic sins
(Half-hinted vice, arcane, unnameable) –
He stretches bedroom slippers to the blaze,
Sinks deeper in the green luxuriant plush,
And bids a comfortable stuffiness
Soothe and allay the thought of six days' toil –
The Toiler now the Lord. The morning slides
Insensibly towards the dinner-hour
When sizzling beef, succulent brussels-sprouts,
And crisp potatoes laved in dense brown gravy
Render material aid to Sunday's heaven
(Yet even these inglorious when the suet,
Doyenne and dowager of puddings, comes!) ...
Next, the ineffable replete siesta,
Sacrosanct doze from 2 till 4 p.m.,
With dreams of angels, strangely like the chorus
Of the Kilburn Empire grand revue last week,
Who bear him up to even happier realms ...
But waking draws a veil too soon, too soon,
And tea-time. Yet hot muffins have their balm
Even for the wakened sleeper ... Now a walk
Through darkening streets, past friendly public-houses,
Past where from windows of fried-fish-shops steal
Ribbons of steam that wreathe and thinly curdle,
Wafting their odour to the passing nose.
Then home to supper and the evening pipe:
Wireless (London, Daventry): and then
(Glorious procrastination!) gradually,
Grumblingly, regally, at length to bed.

Nightfall

Silkily stroking out the grasses
The wind passes,
Leaving them peaceful, slaked
By his caresses.

The clouds lie stretched at rest,
Their lover the sun being gone, their love burnt out;
And, passion sated,
Sleep.

The winds, their search abated, keep
Asylum in the hills' soft breast.

And there is hush and surcease of all zest.

Do you too rest,
And of these tears now
No more!
For see, Love,
To-night there is no footsore, weary moon;
Only a steadfast star.

Winter evening

Frost holds the land, and hollow
Grinds the wheel of stars.
The north wind's ebb tide hisses
Back from earth's iron shores.

The cold's rust bites the metal
Of branch, unpetalled stalk.
A red moon hangs and crackles,
Caught in the half dead oak.

Misty morning on Chelsea Embankment

The mist enshrouding all,
Things have beginnings but not ends.
The bridge is a span launched into space
And there arrested –
A lance shot without aim.
Each stretch of the road
Is a possibility;
The mist's grey veils
Are continued renewals of mystery.
The too quotidian sureness
Of our world seems now withdrawn a little
Into the chaos of creation,
The original womb of doubt.

'Œdipus' at the New Theatre, 1945

Their eyes are dry
    Of tears' relief
And mouth gapes black
    A mask of grief
And body bends
    Thin as a leaf.

And inch by inch
    The shades close in
For the hard gods strike
    The innocent sin
And only the gods
    In the end can win.

The city: midday nocturne

The yellow sky
hangs low its awning
on the city spires.

Herded buses
edge through the gloom
with blunt noses.

        A policeman's white forearm

            semaphores slowly.

The men in black coats
who advance up Ludgate Hill
bend their faces
and wonder if this
is the end of the world
at last?

Winter, 1939–40

Those of us (short of sight,
You say and may be right;
No leaders certainly)
Who find that we can see
No path, no pattern, and
Hardly beyond our hand,
May at least not-let-go
The little that we know,
The little that we have
Of warm and personal love:
May hold what shred we can
Of individual man.

Apologia

If my heart is bound
to no abiding bliss,
but if I find random happiness
in many times and places –
am I thereby the poorer?

If I live a fortuitous and wholly
unsystematic sort of life,
that affords no theme to the biographer,
no subject for an epic:
if I fit into no category,
but derive from all categories
and if I am different men to different men,
and have in me something of all men:
and if I feather my nest in many henroosts,
and dance to many fiddles,
and sit at the feet of many Gamaliels,
– is that a matter for remorse?

If I am neither orthodox nor orthodoxly unorthodox,
walk neither in the rut nor wholly out of it,
am I for this reason to be pitied? ...
If I am inconsistent
am I necessarily insincere?

An untidy affair, I admit, this life of mine,
but not without its illuminations –
the light falling accidentally for a moment just so –
the epigram, *le mot juste*, in actuality –
something that perhaps could not have happened
with a more elaborate *mise-èn-scene*
or otherwise than as a by-product ...
And shall I then complain
at the main piece falling almost invariably flat,
when the sideshows and unrehearsed incidents
revealed such unexpected charm?

Steel April

(to F.G.H.)

You say that our civilisation's a six-foot cage for pampas muscles;
a shearing of Samson's hair (and, if need be, ears) till the cap
      will fit;
the Woolworth watch-chain exchanged by the Birmingham trader
      for ivory and ebony;
the Zulu chieftain in a Whitechapel two-ten ready-made suit.

You say that our civilisation is hasty incompetent filing;
a Tiller troupe filling its gaps from the ranks of the spare Pavlovas;
a musical-comedy chorus of newsboys and opera singers;
Hollywood framing the face of Garbo in sex-for-hicks.

You say that our civilisation is Willesden Green; is Beaverbrook;
Lyons'; halitosis advertisements; cancer and pyorrhœa; prize-day,
      the cheers and avuncular tips for the prudent cheaters;
pearl-divers diving their lungs out; tin-workers breathing in tin.

You say it's the scientist flattering the oil-king; D. H. Lawrence
baited by moral horseflies; starving of Carnevali;
Modigliani killed more slowly than Sacco and Vanzetti;
Yeats grown bitter; Baudelaire with syphilis; Van Gogh mad ...

You're right ... but there's also my civilisation ... somewhere,
      arriving:
the plane long delayed, behind schedule some centuries,
      held up by cloudbanks,
a strut or two broken – but coming: my civilisation advancing
whenever a man gains his claim to work, shirk, without spies
      at the window,
whenever minorities win (though majorities steal their slogans),
whenever a censor's shamed, or an inquisition abolished.

I regret your bohemia's aesthetic blindness to the lovely world
of wavesmooth tyrannous cars and departures in the Golden Arrow
and girls with expensive lips, plucked eyebrows and precise buttocks.
I admire Arnold Bennett's adjustment of such frank appreciations
to the artist's need to be homeless, uprooted, disloyal,
ready with a curt antiseptic finger for entrails, his own or another's.

My civilisation won't backstep to witch-hunting, leeches, plague-years;
will make money light, parachute-like, not end it, or spend it on sandals;
will lubricate, tune the engine, until it is silken-silent;
will make new factories flowers of steel, not flower-façaded;
its men neither slaves to a thirst nor slaves to the quenching fountain;
binding them neither to hardship nor comfort, humility nor pride.

My civilisation is difficult, light and laughing balance;
the step past disillusion; patience for underpinning;
shoring instead of bonfires; organisation allowing
the flourish of grace, beauty's self-waste, blood's stir and surplus, –
giving the rebel a match for his skill, a bone he can get his teeth in, –
turning rebellion to a fanning breath and tradition to a jet of flame.

To the world in the rare intervals between the unveiling of memorials

Up, world! Be quick, world! Crown the head
And flag the sky and raise the cheers,
And say the word that's better said
To open than to earth-stopped ears.
Anticipate your epitaphs
World, before the wise worm laughs.

Thomas Hardy

Our faltering posthumous tributes can only lie ...
Our words, remembering his, are somehow shy ...
Being already immortal – strange he should die!

On the death of a great man

He goes. You, world, are poorer for his going;
And poorer yet again, world, for not knowing
Your loss ... 'Tis well, world. You deserved to lose
That which you neither sought, nor cared to use!

Classics

These – in their lifetimes lothest to conform
To preconception, definition, norm
Drawn from the past by its epigoni –
Resistant to attempt to classify:
These same, now, irremediably immortal,
Stand as unwilling sentries at the portal
Of Art's High Pantheon, that none may pass
Who might foil expectation, flout the mass
Of precedent, ruffle habitual sense,
Or disobey *their* disobedience.

X, while talking to a Professor, wonders whether he shall persuade his daughter to enter upon a University course

Shall I ask this learned porter,
  This dull janitor of shades,
Eruditely to escort her
  Through the dusty colonnades,

Through the echoing halls of culture,
  Where the dead are not allowed
Boon of even brief sepulture,
  But are wrested from the shroud

And by scholarship are harried
  Into neat galvanic drill ...?
Shall he show her every arid
  Phrase in Time's least codicil?

Like the rest, shall she be loaded
  With the Past, the Incubus:
Shall she be admonished, goaded
  By the pious '*They* did *thus*'?

Or shall she be free, unfettered,
  Virgin for the future's kiss? ...
Pundit tell me, do you lettered
  Gain the more, or do you miss

Something not Minerva's giving? ...
  Shall she with this learned one
Seek the dead? – or seek the living?
  Light of lamp, or light of sun?

On listening to
a piece of music by Purcell

I cast no slur upon the worth
Of modern men and modern ways,
And our no whit declining days –
On modern heaven and modern earth;
Yet in your muse I seem to find
Something our later muse has lost –
A note more sure, less trouble-tossed,
A carelessness and ease of mind –

Relic of times when History's ink
Had scrawled less wantonly the page,
When Man had had less time to think,
Less circumspectly flowed his blood:
Trace of a prelapsarian age,
Echo of days before the flood.

Stars may fall in one's hand

When you are with me, I, who am all too sane, am a little mad.
Through you I see colours where yesterday were
        grey, black, white, and tomorrow perhaps grey,
        black, white will be again.
Your eyes reflect impossible towns, trees, flowers,
        inconceivable lights and faces.
Your voice holds incredible echoes of unlikely words.
Your time has no days, hours, minutes;
And all things are possible; And stars, like snow, may fall in one's hand.

Pets

An indoor elephant
Seems irrelevant.
Keeping a seagull
Is not legal.

Armadillos
Nest in pillows.
Hungry llamas
Eat pyjamas.

Hippo and rhino
Damage the lino.
Crocodiles stay
In the bath all day.

Women are flustered
If a large bustard,
Eagle or lion
Watches them iron.

Such birds as grouse
Flap through the house
And polar bears
Block up the stairs.

Sheep are loafers
On chairs and sofas
And few sane men
Can love a hen.

Most people therefore
Prefer to care for
A dog or cat;
And that is that.

Warning to Gloria

I wait for you whose half past six is seven
Or eight – or nine tomorrow: who may someday
Discover clocks as Christopher Columbus
Suddenly saw America. And, waiting,
I say to you who are not here, 'Remember,
I hate your large, magnificent indifference
To time because I love you: hate this waiting
To see and touch and hear you, to be near you.
And one day when you've kept me too long waiting
I may say something which you won't forgive me
Nor I forgive myself; and then, love, then what
Unthinkable ending? Try to think, remember
That love and hate are next-door neighbours meeting
Like day and night, like happiness and tears.'

First meeting

(to Diane)

When I first met you I knew I had come at last home,
Home after wandering, home after long puzzled searching,
Home after long being wind-borne, wave-tossed, night-caught,
Long being lost;

And being with you as normal and needful and natural
As sleeping or waking; and I was myself, who had never
Been wholly myself; I was walking and talking and laughing
Easily at last;

And the air was softer and sounds were sharper
And colours were brighter and the sky was higher
And length was not measured by milestones and time was not
    measured by clocks ...
And this end was a beginning ...
And these words are the beginning of my thanks.

Morning meeting
(for B.B.)

After sick subtle people –
You, with your natural way
Of living, laughing, loving:
After the half-lights, day.

After spoiled plotting people
With minds that fork and twist –
Your clearness, your clean giving:
Sunbreak after mist.

After the sated soiled ones –
You, with your quick direct
Joy and sorrow and anger
Not audited, cross-checked.

After the cunning cold ones
Controlled and old in guile –
You, with your warm body,
Your warm and curling smile.

After cross-weaving shadows
On tired and turning sight –
You for whom I have waited
As eyes for morning light.

Poems hitherto uncollected

Symphony in red

Within the church
The solemn priests advance,
And the sunlight, stained by the heavy windows,
Dyes a yet richer red the scarlet banners
And the scarlet robes of the young boys that bear them,
And the thoughts of one of these are far away,
With carmined lips pouting an invitation,
Are with his love – his love, like a crimson poppy
Flaunting amid prim lupins;
And his ears hear nought of the words sung from the rubricked book,
And his heart is hot as the red sun.

Monochrome

Reine sirène d'or
sun running east under Waterloo Bridge
(entrancing aged trees
that lean over the parapet like old men smiling
    at a golden-haired barmaid)
reine sirène d'or
abdicates into shadows.

In Piccadilly Circus
buses balance themselves
on the slippery plank
they themselves have greased with light.

Lit cigar-ends draw sagging
phosphorescent telegraph wires
past Appenrodt's, round by the Monico, past the Pavilion.

Gymnastic of comets
rococo euclid in fire
Deauville, Schweppes, Gordon's Gin!

[133]

Charleston

Now the saxophones' chattering, spattering
Brazen laughter and banjos' clattering
Under the nimble fingers are witching
The young girls' calves setting itching, twitching
From heel to thigh, setting haunches wagging
Silk knees knocking, rocking, sagging ...
Thicker the saxophones' searing, racking
Asthma, louder the chuckling, clacking
Diabolical laughter grows still –
Outward heels and inward toes, till
Every smooth pink leg is kicking,
Flank quaking, shank shaking, sleek calf flicking ...
While tall dark men in their starched regalia
Join in the negroid Saturnalia,
Black legs flapping against pink to the tweaking
Of banjos' and saxophones' lost-soul-shrieking ...
Till suddenly like water disappearing when the plug
Is drawn the music ebbs away and vanishes glug-glug
And the couples (bubbles burst) relapse from tom-tom jubilation
Into tit-for-tat back-chat and flat conversation.

Man mending telegraph wire

Wire stitching space too loosely
requires that his head be nested
close to the air-singing sheaf,
the delicate maze,
the honeycomb for wind.

The new wire is bright bronze.
It burns in the blue air.
The sun's thread weaves across it.
It rings in the sun.

Soliloquy of the artists

It is our pride to be
Independent as the cat,
Shunning attachments that
Should limit our ubiquity.

The imprisonment of
Property we abhor
But even more
The yet more galling chains of love.

We are (it is our vaunt)
Of no more fixed abode or home
Than Paris, London, Rome
Affords for tent's-pitch, three-nights'-haunt.

We strike no roots:
Assume no preconceived set role:
Seek no shell for the soul:
Are this or that as suits ...

We admire the cat not only
For its independence but for its privacy:
Contrive to be
World-intimate and sedulously lonely: ...

Call nothing sacrosanct:
Spare none, not even ourselves: dissect
All, ourselves most of all: nor expect,
Save after our death, to be thanked.

Dancing

(to J.M.)

Your hands have rituals as old as springtime.
Your hands are birds, climbing the stairs of air.
Your hands are flying silver fish escaping
From what faint shadow, of what threatening, where?

If the octopus ...

If the octopus suddenly feels a wish
To dine on a plump young passing fish
He stays very still and he keeps very calm
And he reaches out arm after arm after arm.

Chelsea Embankment

Like hard knife-blades
the seagulls' wings
carve air.
      Their cries
are sharp.
      The wind
bites.

The housetops
cut the cold sky.

Piccadilly

In Piccadilly
in a maze of hurrying scurrying
men women motorbuses Rolls Royces
no time no time no timetowaste!

but across the road
in the Park
is a world slowed down
where people move doubtfully
as in dreams and with difficulty
under trees that aspire
vaguely
above which
across the thin sky

         a few birds
           zigzag
             one
               by
                 one.

Spring in Hyde Park

The clouds are fluffed hair
  of film-star blondes.
The trees sway
  like Anna May Wong.
In Rotten Row
  men tight-waisted ride
  horses from a Persian miniature
  with voluptuous haunches and cabriole legs.
The Round Pond is dimpled
  only as much as
  a girl's knee.

The conductor (concert study)

His arms are long
tentacles on
the clotted breeze
of brass – catarrhal horns
crackling trombones.
He wafts towards us
(meek rows of waiting faces)
a gust of violins,
a wave that rises, rises
till he too rises on it
and hovers far above us
then falls like a pricked balloon ...
But for a moment he is master.
He bends towards the oboes and the oboes whine
inclines towards the celli and each rich brown belly
        speaks harmonious moans;
to the piccolo and obedient the piccolo squeaks
he coaxes, wheedles, they answer ...
When suddenly all the instruments shout at once
clarinets, trumpets, drums:
tiptoe he strives to quell the clamour
(but triangle and cymbals hammer):
he is overwhelmed; wrestles, again to reel
(hard hails the glockenspiel)
towers once more, once more quails ... and emerges
triumphant from the music's surges:
stands erect, dripping, while the heavens pause:
then crumples as we thunder our applause.

Order

I

Traffic's
two shining rows of beads
are drawn along their two invisible strings

but the policeman's white forearm
scissoring
cuts the string

II

Blue and white semaphore
the policeman simplifies
the world into lines at right angles

just as God has reduced
the cloud and fire of sin
to a spectrum of ten neatly coloured bands.

Conversation with a disembodied spirit

'Soul, you have lips?' 'Lips, as you see,
  To talk with.' 'Can they kiss?'
'They can, but don't. I'm neither he
  Nor she.' 'You're glad of this?'

'I'm neither glad nor sad. I'm free.
  And yet I seem to miss
Something ... as I, reluctantly,
  Look down on earthly bliss.'

Now I shall sing to you ...

Now I shall sing to you, and you,
The few (perhaps the not so few)
For whom some memories remain
Of days we shall not see again ...
Days in a distant, dim November
Long ago. Do you remember ...

Hooves that rang in Piccadilly,
Hansoms rattling in the rain?
Now cabbies and their whips are silent;
Won't be times like those again.

All the stalls agleam with shirtfronts,
Huntley's world and Edna May's,
Monocles and white gardenias ...
Those were definitely days.

No more suppers at Romano's
With Odette or Pearl or Vi.
Stagedoor Johnnies wait no longer.
We were lucky, you and I.

Gone the frills that waltzing, whirling,
Brushed the floor that shone like glass;
Gone the pencil-dangling programmes ...
How the pleasant things can pass.

Lazy lawns and time for croquet,
Housemaids bringing out the tea,
Boaters, blushes, all are vanished ...
Sunny days our sons won't see.

Muffin Man and songs by Tosti,
Gleam of gaslight, flick of fan,
Plushed and mirrored Café Royal,
Gone, and gone for good, old man.

Where are Florrie Ford, Kate Carney,
Ella Retford, Harry Tate,
Marie Lloyd, and Tich and Leno?
Come, drink up ... it's getting late.

Art-galleries

Art-galleries have the musky, uninhabited smell of churches,
the sweet-sour smell of places
where no-one eats, drinks or makes love.

Here is somewhere one should come, one May morning,
    without an appointment,

to warm one's hands before a Gauguin
or to cool them at a Manet
or to sip a Laurençin through a straw;
instead of which one is oneself, a person come to look at pictures
among other people come to look at pictures;
listening to the remarks the deferential do not make
and the stifled coughs of schoolmistresses
and the other silences;
knowing that the soul has paid that spiritual gate-money Time
    at the door
and must account for it this evening, at the audit of dinner,
    to friends.

Here birdsong is caged and rebellion glazed and varnished
by the tactless promiscuity of Fame or the flattery of Death.

Here even the present is past.
Here nothing stirs
but used epigrams tangled in pointing fingers
and eulogies fluttering, unnoticed, to the floor.

The train

In the train
that rolls and blackly crashes
and smears a white fleer of smoke
on the sky, which the sky erases –
in the train's thirty compartments
sit a hundred people whose thoughts
flutter, separately, vaguely,
whose hundred breasts hold close
desires like birds in darkness
clinging to their narrow perches,
hugging their feathers round them
and peering with eyes that have forgotten the light.
But the windows of the train are shut
and if anyone opened them
and opened these breasts
and the birds flew from their perches
they would hardly know where to go in the light that
    blinded their half-shut eyes
and their maimed wings would fail, and they would fall,
    lead-heavy, to the ground.

The pathetic fallacy

Not satisfied to perpetrate
   Magnifications of himself
In iron and steel, and educate
   The savage in desire for pelf,

To prove himself his neighbour's lord,
   And subjugate his fellow-men,
To slay in public with the sword,
   And slay in private with the pen, –

Man further asks that nature shall
   Incline a sympathetic ear,
And at the fitting time let fall
   A warm consolatory tear:

Require Diana to perform
   Her evolutions for his sake,
And, sad, expects the thunderstorm
   To echo to his every ache,

And communes with the earth, and seeks
   A consanguinity in stones,
Apostrophising mountain peaks,
   And plaguing Neptune with his moans, –

Happy if only he rehearse
   His woes to some mute auditor –
This pivot of the universe,
   This egoist, this eternal bore.

Lines

The delicate company of telegraph wires
Frailly banded together,
Progressing on their tall stilts
Up hill and down dale
Endlessly on
And on ...

The road,
Slight ribbon clinging
Closely to the earth's crust,
Sedulously and obediently following its eccentricities,
Hesitating at times at an obstacle,
Fastidiously skirting a pitfall,
Wavering but never retreating,
Bravely surmounting whatever it meets,
And going endlessly on
And on ...

Twin stips of steel
Drawn thin but strong,
Clean-cut,
Across the cross-strips of the sleepers,
Casting a firm even shadow
On the counter-pattern of wood:
Less obedient, more obstinate than the road,
Subjugating, levelling,
Leaving a smooth green hill
Sliced like a cake
With deep brown wound clean-edged,
Flinging a rampart across a gulf,
Leaping a river,
Undermining a mountain,
Its slim parallels going
Endlessly on
And on ...

Earth,
Man has meshed you,
Netted you with his net,
Criss-crossed you across and across,
Patterned you according to his wish,
Subjected you to compass and set-square!

And you too, sea, he has patterned,
Plotting algebraic routes
Whose furrows efface themselves,
Leaving no indent –
A more impermanent geometry.

And you, air –
In your cartography
He is still diffident,
Has as yet but traced upon you
One or two desultory diagrams,
A few tentative strokes!

In that cold land
(to J.M.)

Ghosts do not kiss, or, if they kiss, they feel
Ice touching ice, and turn away, and shiver;
But there as here, perhaps, we still can steal
Quietly off, and talk and talk for ever.

Defence of the ad-man

He brings us aims and dreams and drugs; he tells
Us fairy-tales that half come true or might.
The patent panaceas that he sells
May be placebos, but placebos can
Act like elixirs; syrups have their spells,
And coloured water sometimes can assuage
A thirst for draughts from unattainable wells.

He binds us with a frayed but silver rope.
He peddles jewels false perhaps but bright.
He kindles flares that beckon eyes that grope.
His 'you, you, you' consoles the lonely man
And humble woman. With permitted dope
He medicines the sickness of our age;
Offers the ugly, glamour; the hopeless, hope.

Latterday oracles:
Noise

Listen to me and you will not need to listen
To your own voice thin as a shred of paper uncurling,
Your laughter empty and brittle as an eggshell:
Your thoughts thrown back in your teeth by the cynical wind.

You will not hear the diffidence of breath,
The importunacy of blood, denying death,
The pulse's halt and start,
The morse code of the heart,
Or your two hands whispering together, unquiet as air-stirred leaves.

Listen to me and you will not need to listen.
I am your rampart against silence, time,
And all the gods with empty arms, and eyes
Cold as mirrors, cold and white with questions.

To a lover of living

You demand your life, like your brandy,
Served in balloon glasses.
You demand the full bouquet,
In your warm hands, of today.

You savour life with your tongue-tip's
Inquisitive approbation;
Then drink without fear, without
Reservation of doubt,

Without regret or wonder
When what is over is over,
The glass powdered and flung
By the random wind among

Alien, ancient, lost
And undeciphered dust.

Portrait

She lives continually; she gives incautiously
  With heart, mind, senses.
She builds no walls around her save
  Those final fences

Within whose ring her inmost self, a fiery foal,
  Curvets and paces –
High-mettled, shy, recalcitrant
  To bits and traces.

And he who hopes to catch that soul, that foal, must have
  So patient, clever
A hand, must be so young and old
  And wise a lover!

A painting by Seurat

('Un dimanche à la Grande Jatte')

They rustle in stiff silk skirts:
regimented into the bodice,
tortured into the bustle;
their shape a reversed question-mark
interrogating the past,
and finding nothing to regret ...
and at their sides the attendant males,
in sombre mourning for their lost innocence,
the tall hat pressing upon their foreheads
as the sense of respectability upon their minds;
the gold watch fortifying the fickle heart,
the high collar restraining the curious neck ...
And, finally, sad trailing children,
and sycophantic dogs.

So,
to and fro –
etiolated spectres ...
And above the susurrus of skirts
you can almost hear the response
of heart to throbbing heart, ...
but the mind disapproves
the indecorum even
of interest ...
and they pass on – the spectres –
separate,
envious ...

That lady there,
looking into the water,
tall like a lavender stalk:
who knows what tragedy transpires
beneath that wasp-like waist!

Man

I, vulnerable frail thing,
(in my self nothing:
yet a fulcrum,
a focus)
stand
upon the precarious pin-point of today,
and project into the blank void of tomorrow
shadows of yesterday.

Authorship

The cold-blood committal
of the heart's pangs
to documents:
the transpiration of the soul
in public:
the embodiment
of the innermost self
in a neat collocation
of black signs on white paper
to be coolly perused
by promiscuous laughing strangers –
words capable of being recited
in an infinite number of ways
but especially satirically ...
when I consider the bravery of it
I sympathise with those
who anticipate ridicule by self-ridicule;
but I admire perhaps most
those who romantically fling the gage
full in the blear public eye
with a frank be-damned-to-you.

Sleep: II

Downward
    downward
        fall
           fold
              inward
                  inward
                      feathers
                          soft
                            ah soft
                              ah so
                                so
                              sleep!

Translations from the French
of Jacques Prévert

Pater noster

(Pater noster)

Our Father which art in Heaven
Stay there
And for our part we'll stay on the earth
Which is often so delightful
With its mysteries of New York
And its mysteries of Paris
Which are just as puzzling as the mystery of the Trinity
With its
And its Great Wall of China
Its
And its
Its Pacific Ocean
And its two ponds at the Tuileries
Its good children and bad types
With all the wonders of the world
Which are simply there
There on the earth
Ready for everybody
Spread right out
Wondering at themselves for being such wonders
And not daring to admit their wonder
Like a pretty girl who doesn't dare to show her nakedness
With all the unspeakable sorrows of the world
Which are legion
With their legionaries
And their executioners
With the bosses of this world
The bosses and their bishops and their blackguards and their bullies
With the seasons
With the years
With the pretty girls and the old hags
With the rags of poverty rotting among the bright new guns
fed into the mouths of guns

Song of the snails who go to the funeral

(Chanson des escargots qui vont à l'enterrement)

Two snails are setting out
For the funeral of a leaf
The shells they wear are black
They've crêpe tied round their horns
They are setting out in the darkness
Of a very fine autumn evening
But alas when they arrive
It is already Spring
And so the dry dead leaves
Are all alive again
And the two black solemn snails
Are very disappointed
But look there is the sun
The sun that says to them
Come make yourselves at home
Come friends please take a seat
And take a glass of beer
And if you're so inclined
Come take the Paris bus
It starts at eight this evening
You'll see the countryside
But don't don't mourn my friends
Come take this tip from me
Black doesn't suit the complexion
It's dreadfully unbecoming
This talk of shrouds and coffins
Is terribly depressing
Dear friends be your natural colour
The natural colour of life
And then the whole concourse of animals
And trees and flowers and plants
Suddenly start to sing

To sing for all they're worth
To sing the song of life
To sing the song of summer
And everyone starts drinking
Drinking each other's health
And the evening's a wonderful evening
A wonderful summer evening
And at last the two black snails
Decided to start for home
They go off full of emotion
They go off full of happiness
And having had plenty to drink
They're a little unsteady on their feet
But high in the sky the moon
The watching moon protects them

First day

(Premier jour)

White sheets in a cupboard
Red sheets in a bed
The child in its mother
The mother in her pain
The father in the passage
The passage in the house
The house in the city
The city in the night
And death in a cry
And the child in life

The broken mirror
(Le miroir brisé)

The little man who sang without end
the little man who danced in my head
the little man whose name was youth
broke the lace of his shoe
and all the tents of the fair
suddenly fell down there
and there in the silence of that fair
in the desert of that head of mine
I heard your happy voice
your torn and tenuous voice
your childish disconsolate voice
come out of the distance and call to me
and I put my hand on my heart
where stirred
blood-spattered
the seven mirror-splinters of your star-shivered laugh

The bunch of flowers
(Le bouquet)

What are you doing little girl
With those fresh-cut opening flowers
What are you doing young girl
With those wilting wilting flowers
What are you doing pretty woman
With those flowers that are fading
What are you doing old woman
With those flowers that are dying

I am waiting for the conqueror to come

He circled round me

(Il a tourné autour de moi)

He circled round me
for months days hours
and he put his hand on my breast
calling me his own dear heart
And he dragged a promise out of me
as you drag a flower out of the earth
And he kept this promise in his hand
as you keep a flower under glass
I forgot my promise
and the flower immediately faded
And his eyes started out of his head
he gave me dirty looks
and he said hard hurtful things
Then another came along who asked for nothing
but he looked me through and through
For him I was already naked
from head to feet
and when he undressed me
I let be I let go
And who he was I didn't care or know

Paris by night

(Paris at night)

Three matches in the night lit one by one
The first to see your whole face
The second to see your eyes
The last to see your mouth
And then deep darkness to let me remember it all
As I hold you in my arms

For you my love

(Pour toi mon amour)

I went to the marketplace where they sell birds
And I bought some birds
For you
my love
I went to the marketplace where they sell flowers
And I bought some flowers
For you
my love
I went to the marketplace where they sell old iron
And I bought some chains
Some heavy chains
For you
my love
Then I went to the market place where they sell slaves
And I looked for you there
But I did not find you there
my love

The birds of sorrow

(Les oiseaux du souci)

Rainfall of feathers feathers of falling rain
She who loved you will never come back again
What do you want of me birds
Feathers of falling rain oh rainfall of feathers
Now that my love won't come any more I don't know any more
I don't know where I'm going and nothing is plain
Rainfall of feathers feathers of falling rain
I don't know any longer what to do
Pall of black rain of rain that falls like pain
Can it be true that never again
Pall-black feathers ... Away with you swallows be off now
Get out of your nests ... What's that? Not time to start yet?
To hell with time get out of this room you swallows of morning
Swallows of evening go ... Go where? No no it's I who'll go
Feathers of darkness darkness of feathers I'll go go nowhere anywhere go
So stay here birds of despair
Stay ... make yourselves at home

Quicksands

(Sables mouvants)

Torments and wonders
Winds and tides
Now already the sea has withdrawn
And you
Like a strand of seaweed gently caressed by the wind
In the shoals of the bed you are stirring and dreaming
Torments and wonders
Winds and tides
Now already the sea has withdrawn
But there in your half-awake eyes
Are lingering two small waves
Torments and wonders
Winds and tides
Two small waves waiting to drown me soon

When children are in love

(Les enfants qui s' aiment)

When children are in love they make love standing
In the doorways of the night
And when passers-by go past they point them out
But children in love
Aren't there for anyone else
And it's only their shadow
That flickers in the night
Arousing the anger of passers-by
Their anger their scorn their laughter their envy
Children in love aren't there for anyone else
They are somewhere much further away than night
Much higher than the sky above
In the blinding light of their first love

Song of the gaoler

(Chanson du geolier)

Where are you going brave gaoler
With that key that is stained with blood
I am going to free the one I love
If there's still time
The one I've imprisoned
Tenderly cruelly
In the deep dark dungeon of my desire
In the dark cell of my anguish
In the lies of the future
In the folly of promises
I want to deliver her
I want her to be free
And even to forget me
And even to go away
And even to come back
And to love me again
Or to love someone else
If she needs someone else
And if I am left alone
And she gone away
I shall only keep
I shall always keep
In my two hollowed hands
To the end of my days
The smoothness of her breasts that were shaped by love

Food for thought

(La grasse matinée)

It's a terrible thing
the small noise of a hard-boiled egg being cracked on a metal counter
when it rings in the memory
the mind of a hungry man
and it's a terrible thing the face of the man
the face of the man who is hungry
when he looks at himself at six in the morning
in the glass of the big shop window
and sees a face the colour of dust
yet it isn't his head that he looks at
in the grocer's window
he doesn't care a damn for that human head of his
doesn't give it a thought
he dreams
he has a vision of another head
a calf's head perhaps
with vinegar sauce
or any sort of head that can be eaten
and gently he moves his jaws
very gently
and gently he grinds his teeth
for the world is laughing at him laughing its head off
he counts on his fingers one two three
one two three
it's three days since he has eaten
and it's no good telling and telling himself for three days
It can't go on
for it does go on
three days
three nights
without eating
and behind these shop windows

are these pies these bottles these jars
these dead fish protected by tins
these tins protected by windows
these windows protected by policemen
these policemen protected by men's fear
what fortifications for six unfortunate sardines! ...
A little further on is the café
coffee-and-cream and fresh rolls
the man lurches along
and inside his head
a cloud of words
a cloud of words
sardines on toast
hard-boiled egg coffee and cream
coffee with a dash of rum
coffee and cream
coffee and cream
coffee and crime with a dash of blood! ...
a man well-thought-of in his neighbourhood
has had his throat cut in broad daylight
the murderer robbed him of
one and ten
that's one coffee with a dash of rum
at a shilling
and two buttered rolls
and twopence for the waiter's tip

It's a terrible thing
the small noise of a hard-boiled egg
being cracked on a metal counter
it's a terrible noise
when it rings in the memory
the mind of a hungry man

This love

(Cet amour)

This love
So violent
So vulnerable
So tender
So desperate
This love
Beautiful as the morning
And stormy as the sky
When the sky is stormy
This love so real
This love so beautiful
So happy
So joyful
And so tantalising
Shivering with fright like a child in the dark
And so sure of itself
Like a man at peace in the middle of the night
This love that scared other people
That made them talk
That made them turn pale
This love they watched
Because we watched them
This love that was harried wounded trampled killed denied
    forgotten by others
Because it was harried wounded trampled killed denied
    forgotten by us
This love so complete still
So alive still
So sun-lit-shining
It's yours
It's mine

Something that has happened
That's always new
That has never changed
That's real as a plant
Easily hurt as a bird
Warm and living as summer
And we can both go away
And come back
We can forget
And fall asleep
Wake suffer grow old
And fall asleep again
And dream of death
And wake and smile and laugh
And grow young again
For our love is still there
Obstinate as a mule
Living as desire
Cruel as memory
Foolish as regret
Tender as recollection
Cold as marble
Beautiful as morning
Vulnerable as a child
It looks at us and smiles
And talks to us without saying a word
And I listen and I am afraid
And I cry out
I cry out for you
I cry out for myself
I plead with you
For you for me for all who are in love
And who are loved

Yes I cry out to love
For you for me for all the rest
Whom I don't know
Stay oh stay
There where you are
There where you were before
Stay oh stay
Don't ever move
Don't go away
We who are loved
We have forgotten you
But don't forget us
You are all we have in the world
Don't let us grow cold
Don't go further and further away
And wherever you may be
Show us that you are still alive
One distant day at the edge of a thicket
In the forest of memory
Rise up suddenly and
Hold out your hand
And save us

I am just what I am

(Je suis comme je suis)

I am just what I am
I'm made the way I'm made
And when I want to laugh
I laugh to wake the dead
I like men who like me
And is it yet a crime
If a girl doesn't like
The same man every time
I am just what I am
I'm made like that you see
And what more do you want
What do you want of me

I'm made for pleasing men
And I can't change it now
My heels are much too high
My breasts are much too round
My body's much too curved
My eyes are too dark-ringed
          And anyhow
What's it to you all this
I am just what I am
I please the men I please

What's it to do with you
What has happened to me
Yes I've loved somebody
And somebody's loved me
We've loved as children love
Just knowing how to love
          And love and love ...
But skip the why and how
I'm here to please you men
And I can't change it now

The dunce

(Le cancre)

He says no with his head
but he says yes with his heart
he says yes to things he likes
he says no to the teacher
he is standing
he is being questioned
and all the problems are set
suddenly a gust of laughter shakes him
and he rubs out everything
the figures and the words
the dates and the names
the tests and the traps
and in spite of the schoolmaster
and the catcalls of the infant prodigies
with chalks of many colours
on the blackboard of sorrow
he draws the face of joy

The garden

(Le jardin)

Thousands and thousands of years
Wouldn't be enough
To describe
The small second of eternity
In which you kissed me
In which I kissed you
In the Parc Montsouris in Paris
In Paris
On the earth
The earth which is a star

Osiris,
or
the flight into Egypt
(Osiris ou la fuite en Égypte)

It is wartime and summer
Already summer still wartime
And the torn tired town
Still smiles and smiles
With its gentle summer face
Gently smiles at people in love
It is wartime and summer
A man and a woman together
Are walking through an art gallery
Their footsteps are the only footsteps in the empty art gallery
The art gallery is the Louvre
The town is Paris
And the world's morning-freshness
Is fast asleep
An attendant wakes at the sound of the footsteps
Presses a button and sinks back into his dream
While in a niche appears
The wonder of Egypt bathed in light
The figure of Osiris the dead wood alive
Alive enough to make
The dead idols in all the churches of Paris
Die again
And so the lovers kiss
Osiris marries them
And steps back into the shadow
Of his living night

To paint the portrait of a bird

(Pour faire le portrait d'un oiseau)

Paint first a cage
with an open door
paint next
something pretty
something simple
something beautiful
something useful
for the bird
then set up the canvas against a tree
in a garden
in a wood
or in a forest
and hide behind the tree
without saying a word
without moving ...
There are times when the bird arrives quickly
but just as often it is many long years
before it decides
So do not lose heart
just wait
wait if need be for years
the quickness or slowness of arrival
of the bird having no connection
with the merit of the painting
When the bird arrives
if it does arrive
keep the deepest silence
and wait till the bird goes into the cage
and when it is in
shut the door very gently with the brush
then one by one wipe out the bars of the cage
taking care not to touch any of the feathers of the bird

After that paint the portrait of the tree
choosing carefully the loveliest of its branches
for the bird
Paint the greenness of the leaves and the coolness of the wind
the gold-dust of the sunshine
and the noise of the creatures in the grass in the warmth
    of the summer
and then wait for the bird to decide it will sing
If the bird does not sing
that is a bad sign
but if the bird decides to sing it is a good sign
a sign that you can sign
and you pull out very gently
one of the feathers of the bird
and in a corner of the painting you write your name

Unrestricted area

(Quartier libre)

I put my khaki cap in the cage
and went out with the bird on my head
Ha
the army no longer salutes
asked the major
No
the army no longer salutes
answered the bird
Oh
forgive me I thought the army still saluted
said the major
You're entirely forgiven anyone can make a mistake
said the bird

I saw a good many of them ...

(J'en ai vu plusieurs ...)

I saw one of them who had sat on another one's hat
he was pale
he was trembling
he was waiting for something ... anything ...
war ... the end of the world ...
it was utterly impossible for him to move so much as his hand
or to speak
and the other one
the one who was looking for 'his' hat
was even paler
and he too was trembling
and saying to himself again and again:
my hat ... my hat ...
and he wanted to weep
I saw one of them who was reading the papers
I saw one of them who was saluting the flag
I saw one of them who was dressed in black
he had a watch
a watch-chain
a purse
the legion of honour
and pince-nez
I saw one of them who was dragging his child by the hand
and shouting ...
I saw one of them with a dog
I saw one of them with a sword-stick
I saw one of them who was weeping
I saw one of them who was going into a church
I saw another who was coming out ...

The road-sweeper (a ballet)
(Le balayeur)

By the side of a river
the road-sweeper sweeps
he is rather bored
he looks at the sun
he thinks about love
Two linked lovers pass
he follows them with his eyes
The lovers disappear
he sits down on a large stone
But suddenly the music
the tune of the day
which till now was delightful and gentle
becomes menacing
and harsh

Now appears
the road-sweeper's Guardian Angel
who with a very simple gesture
reproaches him for his laziness
and advises him to start work again

The Guardian Angel raises his forefinger to the sky
and disappears
The road-sweeper starts again to sweep

A pretty woman comes along
and leans on the parapet
and looks at the river
She has her back to him
and the position suits her

The road-sweeper makes no sound
but leans beside her
and with a warm and timid hand
caresses her

or rather simply pretends to caress her
imitating the gestures of the man who just now was caressing
    his girl as he walked

The woman goes away without seeing him
He is alone with his brush
and suddenly he realises
that the Angel has come back
and has seen him
and is blaming him
with a gesture more and more affectionate
and more and more menacing
The road-sweeper takes up his brush again
and sweeps
The Guardian Angel disappears

Another woman passes
He stops his sweeping
and with a gesture that says it all
talks to her about the rain
and the sun
and the beauty that is hers
and hers alone

The Angel appears
The woman runs away scared

The Angel yet again
impresses on the road-sweeper
that he is there to sweep
and disappears

The road-sweeper takes up his brush again

Suddenly cries
appeals for help
rising from the river
Without a doubt
the cries of somebody who is drowning

The road-sweeper drops his brush
But suddenly shrugs his shoulders
and
indifferent to the cries rising from the river
goes on sweeping

The Guardian Angel appears
And the road-sweeper sweeps
as he never swept before
Careful irreproachable technique

But the Angel with his forefinger ever raised to the sky
waves angry wings
and makes it clear to the road-sweeper
that it's all very well
to sweep
but all the same
there is somebody
who is quite possibly in the act of drowning
And he insists
the road-sweeper turning a deaf ear

Finally
the road-sweeper takes off his vest
because he can hardly do otherwise
And as he is an extremely good swimmer
he climbs on to the parapet
and dives like an angel
and disappears
And the Angel
praises the Lord
literally to the skies

The music is a music
incontestably celestial

Suddenly
the road-sweeper emerges
carrying in his arms
the person he has saved

It is a very beautiful girl
with no clothes on

The Angel gives him a nasty look

The road-sweeper
lays her on a bench
with infinite delicacy
and cares for her
cherishes her
caresses her

The Angel intervenes
and advises the road-sweeper
to throw back into the river
this 'she-devil'

The 'she-devil' who is regaining a taste for life
thanks to the road-sweeper's caresses
rises
and smiles

The road-sweeper also smiles
They both dance

The Angel threatens them with fire from heaven

They burst out laughing
kiss
and go off dancing

The Guardian Angel wipes away a tear
picks up the brush
and sweeps ... and sweeps ... and sweeps ... and sweeps
in-ex-or-ably

Family group

(Familiale)

The mother has her knitting
The son has his fighting
She finds this quite natural the mother does
And the father has what has the father got?
He has his business
His wife has her knitting
His son his fighting
And he his business
He thinks this quite natural the father does
And the son and the son
What does the son make of this?
He makes precisely nothing does the son
The son's mother has her knitting his father his business
    and he his fighting
And when he has finished his fighting
He will go to business with his father
The fighting goes on the mother goes on knitting
The father goes on going to business
The son is killed he doesn't go on
The father and the mother go to the funeral
They find this quite natural the father and mother do
Life goes on life with knitting fighting business
Business fighting knitting fighting
Business business business
Life and the business of funerals

Despair is sitting on a bench
(Le désespoir est assis sur un banc)

In a square on a bench
There is a man who calls to you as you pass
He wears pince-nez and an old grey suit
He smokes a small cigar as he sits
And he calls to you as you pass
Or he just makes a sign to you
You must not look at him
You must not listen to him
You must pass
Pretend you don't see him
Pretend you don't hear him
You must pass with quickened pace
If you look at him
If you listen to him
He makes a sign to you and nothing and no-one
Can stop you from going to sit next to him
Then he looks at you and smiles
And you suffer horribly
And the man goes on smiling
And you smile the same smile
Precisely
The more you smile the more you suffer
Horribly
The more you suffer the more you smile
Helplessly
And you stay there
Sitting frozen
Smiling on the bench
Children play round you
People pass by
Calmly

Birds fly away
Leaving one tree
For another
And you stay there
On the bench
And you know and you know
That never again will you play
Like these children
You know that never again will you pass
Calmly
Like the others passing
That never again will you fly away
Leaving one tree for another
Like the birds

It is inadvisable ...

(Il ne faut pas ...)

It is inadvisable to let intellectuals play with matches
Because Gentlemen when you leave it by itself
The mental aristocracy Gen-tle-men
Is not at all brilliant
And the moment it's by itself
It behaves high-handedly
And erects to and for itself
With self-styled benevolence in honour of the builders' workmen
A self-monument
Let us emphasize Gen-tle-men
When you leave it alone
The mental aristocracy
Talks monumental
Nonsense

INDEX OF FIRST LINES